Subprime Consumer Lending

Edited by

Frank J. Fabozzi
Adjunct Professor of Finance
School of Management
Yale University

Robert Paul Molay
Consultant

Published by Frank J. Fabozzi Associates

 © Copyright 1999 by Frank J. Fabozzi Associates
New Hope, Pennsylvania

Cover design by Robert Paul Molay

ALL RIGHTS RESERVED. No part of this publication may be reproduced, stored in a retrieval system, or transmitted, in any form or by any means, electronic, mechanical, photocopying, recording, or otherwise without the prior written permission of the publisher and the copyright holder.

This publication is designed to provide accurate and authoritative information in regard to the subject matter covered. It is sold with the understanding that the publisher is not engaged in rendering legal, accounting, or other professional services.

ISBN: 1-883249-78-3

Printed in the United States of America

Table of Contents

1. **Prudent Lending Practices and Nonprime Credit Risk** 2
   Virgil G. Baker, Jr.
2. **Risk-Based Pricing**
   Scott C. Calahan 14
3. **Subprime Collection Methodology**
   Daniel H. Relf 28
4. **Credit Scoring and Risk-Adjusted Pricing:
   A Review of Techniques**
   Craig Allen 40
5. **Credit Card Servicing for the Subprime Market**
   John A. Costa 78
6. **Subprime Automobile Financing**
   Adrian Katz 96
7. **Subprime Auto Paper: Promised Land or Nightmare?**
   Cliff Grubbs 118
8. **Home Equity Loans**
   Leonard Blum 130
9. **Risk-Based Pricing Nonagency Mortgages and Securities**
   Frank L. Raiter 144
10. **FASIT Flexibility Applied to Subprime Securitizations**
    Phillip R. Pollock and Michael E. Shaff 154
11. **Evolution of Subprime Mortgage Lending
    In the United Kingdom**
    Mallory P. Hill 166

   Index 180

Contributing Authors

Craig Allen	Delphi Structured Finance Corp.
Virgil G. Baker, Jr.	Virgil G. Baker & Associates
Leonard Blum	Westwood Capital, LLC
Scott C. Calahan	Boston Portfolio Advisors, Inc.
John A. Costa	Cardholder Management Services, LP
Cliff Grubbs	Primus Automotive Financial Services, a division of Ford Motor Credit Co.
Mallory P. Hill	Mortgages, PLC
Adrian Katz	Autobond Acceptance Corp.
Phillip R. Pollock	Tobin & Tobin
Frank L. Raiter	Standard & Poor's
Michael E. Shaff	Jeffers, Wilson, Shaff & Falk, LLP
Daniel H. Relf	Aames Financial Corp.

Preface

The subprime consumer lending market is growing rapidly and steadily. For a variety of economic reasons, each passing year leaves more and more consumers with some blemish on their borrowing history. Yet the days are gone when an applicant needed a good credit history in order to get a loan.

As noted recently in *The New York Times*, "The traditional rules for lending have softened significantly, particularly with respect to mortgages and home equity loans. Now, credit experts say, borrowers who are already in debt are often welcome to borrow more. And those whose track records have been less than perfect — even abysmal — are often given another chance to prove themselves good bets as borrowers."*

Along with residential mortgage and home equity loans, subprime consumer lending includes major components of automobile loans and credit card receivables.

This book is intended for readers whose professional responsibilities or board memberships require a working, up-to-date knowledge of subprime consumer lending. It provides a guide through the concept of credit risk as it relates to prudent lending practices, risk-based and risk-adjusted pricing, credit scoring, collection methodology, credit card servicing, auto loans, several aspects of the securitization of subprime assets, and recent developments in the United Kingdom. All the authors are active participants in the subprime market.

Prudent Lending Practices and Nonprime Credit Risk, by Virgil G. Baker, Jr., emphasizes the need to plan thoughtfully for long-range growth before entering the nonprime lending arena. Looking back at failures in the nonprime automobile consumer lending marketplace, Baker finds that poor planning and neglect played a major role in their demise: "Management failed to hire the correct people, devote the time necessary to train them properly, and implement underwriting programs that recognized the overall credit risks of the nonprime marketplace."

---

*Jay Romano, "Lenders Softening the Rules," *The New York Times*, December 20, 1998.

Risk-Based Pricing, by Scott C. Calahan, states the case for a predictive approach. He reviews winning — and losing — concepts for measuring and predicting lender risk, and pricing accordingly. Calahan carefully distinguishes past (historic) risk from future (predictive) risk. With regard to historic risk, Calahan comments, "As the old wag said, all of our knowledge is about the past and all of our decisions are about the future. While we can study to death the past, it may or may not look like the future. If the past has been 'ugly,' we want to develop pricing and product strategies that induce change and result in superior performance."

Subprime Collection Methodology, by Daniel H. Relf, accepts the fact that, overall, the subprime portfolio consists of loans with differing degrees of credit blemish — from the occasional late payment on unsecured consumer credit to the severest of credit problems. But his collection strategy is based, in part, on the fact that even prime portfolios contain a certain segment of loans that have become chronic or recurring delinquents. Relf points out: "Every loan portfolio — no matter how it is characterized — has a subprime component that represents a formidable challenge to mortgage loan servicers."

Credit Scoring and Risk-Adjusted Pricing: A Review of Techniques, by Craig Allen, introduces the reader to the quantitative assessment of creditworthiness and predictive credit modeling. The goal for lenders, from Allen's perspective, is somehow to measure a potential borrower and, from that initial assessment, make predictions about the borrower's expected behavior. The obstacle faced by any credit-scoring methodology, according to Allen, "consists first in framing the problem and then determining which borrowers are, for these purposes, similar to one another."

Credit Card Servicing for the Subprime Market, by John A. Costa, begins with a review of the vibrant and disparate credit card marketplace that has evolved for consumers with either poor credit or no credit history. Subprime credit card servicing, as Costa relates it, is the story of how people outside of the traditional economy move into the mainstream of economic life. "Subprime credit cards and other forms of subprime lending are symptoms of economic optimism by an emerging or recovering class." Costa points out that a credit card has utility beyond its lending function: A subprime credit card is primarily an access device — and only secondarily a loan.

Subprime Automobile Financing, by Adrian Katz, points out that there are approximately $600 billion of sales of automobiles each year, for which about 40% of American consumers have some form of credit impairment that could prevent them from obtaining prime automobile financing. Figures cited by Katz suggest that the annual subprime automobile finance activity could exceed $200 billion.

Subprime Auto Paper: Promised Land or Nightmare? by Cliff Grubbs, predicts that subprime paper may retain a strong appeal entering the 21st century because the fundamentals exist for a sound investment program. Grubbs points out that certain financial products seem to come full cycle every four or five years and create the expectation of unparalleled returns: "In an epoch when most A auto receivables were earning minimal yields or getting gobbled up by the securitization types, subprime auto paper jumped to the top of the list in the resurgence of high-return investments. Those who have been in the field for at least the decade of the 1990s will recall that subprime paper had been at the top of this list before, and also at the bottom."

Home Equity Loans, by Leonard Blum, reviews the various features of home-equity loans and explores the dynamics of what has been one of the fastest-growing areas of the HEL market: the nonprime credit (B&C) sector. The HEL allows a homeowner to tap his or her embedded home equity, in return for which the originator is granted a lien on that borrower's residence. Home-equity loans can be either lines of credit (HELOCs) or closed-end (HELs). Within these broad groupings, loans have a wide variety of credit, prepayment, contractual characteristics, and lien positions (first, second, or other.)

Risk-Based Pricing Nonagency Mortgages and Securities, by Frank L. Raiter, traces recent developments in the evaluation of individual loans for residential mortages. As another portent in the technological revolution that is described in detail elsewhere in this book, in the chapter by Craig Allen, Raiter discusses advances in statistical scoring, along with technical improvements in data accumulation and systems, have made risk-based mortgage pricing objective, consistent, speedy, and efficient.

FASIT Flexibility Applied to Subprime Securitizations, by Phillip R. Pollock and Michael E. Shaff, discusses the financial asset securitization Investment trust (FASIT) as a route to greater flexibility in structuring subprime asset securitizations. "The enhanced structuring possibilities created by FASITs can be important in maximizing the efficiency of subprime securitizations, from the issuer's standpoint." Efficiency, as these authors define it, can be measured by the relative amount of proceeds received by the issuer at closing from a given amount of collateral. And, they say, "The more efficient the transaction, relatively speaking, the more proceeds will be realized by the issuer and/or relatively lower levels of collateral will be required."

Evolution of Subprime Mortgage Lending in the United Kingdom, by Mallory P. Hill, notes that the U.K. residential mortgage market, with a common language and lender-friendly laws, beckons U.S. mortgage finance companies seeking additional markets abroad. "As a natural outgrowth of mortgage finance as conducted in North America and the efficient market developed there, the United Kingdom represents growth opportunities due to a number of factors, including its proximity to Europe," Hill maintains: "The timing appears good in the United Kingdom, as values today represent a relative low point in the real estate valuation cycle."

Steve Glener of Information Management Network, who has produced numerous conferences on aspects of subprime consumer lending, helped immeasurably by making initial contact with most of the authors herein.

Frank J. Fabozzi
Editor and Publisher

Robert Paul Molay
Consultant

Virgil G. Baker, Jr., is president and founder of Virgil Baker & Associates, credit underwriters. The company, founded in 1985, has gained a national reputation in analyzing the risk management capabilities of originators and servicers as a prerequisite to securitization activities.

The company's expertise in consumer, mortgage lending, leasing, and factoring has been used by originators, servicers, insurance companies, investment banks, and investors in conjunction with over $35 billion in asset-related transactions.

The firm has consulted with groups across the country on loan origination and servicing improvement strategies, loss control, asset recovery, and has considerable expertise in designing credit risk management programs.

In addition, Baker has authored articles for trade magazines and financial publications, and has been quoted in *Barrons Financial* weekly, *Working Woman* magazine, and *Business Age* magazine. He also served as the external management consultant to a regional financial institution trade group for a number of years.

Previously, Baker was regional vice president, a market-merchandising manager, credit bond department head, and financial analyst, all within the Foremost Corporation of America group; a vice president of a commercial bank; an owner-operator of a small business; and served as the interim general manager of a large full-service financial institution.

A graduate of Aquinas College, Northwestern Michigan College, and the Northern Michigan School of Banking, Baker has also participated in numerous continuing education programs in finance, insurance, marketing, and risk management.

Chapter 1

Prudent Lending Practices And Nonprime Credit Risk

Virgil G. Baker, Jr.
President
Virgil Baker & Associates

The decision to enter the nonprime lending arena needs, first and foremost, to be part of a well-thought-out plan for long-range growth. Generally speaking, failure to approach the market in this way usually spells disaster. A look back at the failures in the nonprime automobile consumer lending marketplace, and the differences between plans and performance, leads to the conclusion that plans that failed were candidates for success only in the minds of the executives who gave birth to them. For the most part, these plans were destined to fail (based on plan implementation reviews conducted after their failure).

Studies conducted by rating agencies and investment banking houses, and independent research into the causes of nonprime lending failures, all support the theory (directly or indirectly) that poor planning and neglect played a major role in their demise. In other words, management failed to hire the correct people, devote the time necessary to train them properly, and implement underwriting programs that recognized the overall credit risks of the nonprime marketplace.

MARKET SITUATION

On a macro basis, the strategy an originator will use to control the credit risk (that is, extending credit regardless of the asset type) is related to certain conditions that exist in the marketplace. Although numerous definitions of risk could be used for purposes of this analysis, they will be classified into two basic segments — those risks associated with a stable or declining market, and those common to a market that is expanding.

The economic issues that may be driving either segment of risk, while important, need not impede the normal expansion or contraction of the extension of credit by a nonprime lender. Those same economic issues do, however, present the opportunity to originate portfolios that can be detrimental to the long-term survival of the originator.

4   Subprime Consumer Lending

Exhibit 1 depicts the situation that exists with regard to overall credit risk and the acceptable credit risk therein, based on predetermined creditworthiness and loan-underwriting standards. The diagram does not make any allowances for a lender's appetite for risk in any one category, other than defining creditworthiness as either high or low and loan-underwriting standards on a continuum from very conservative to very liberal.

Exhibit 1: The Credit Risk

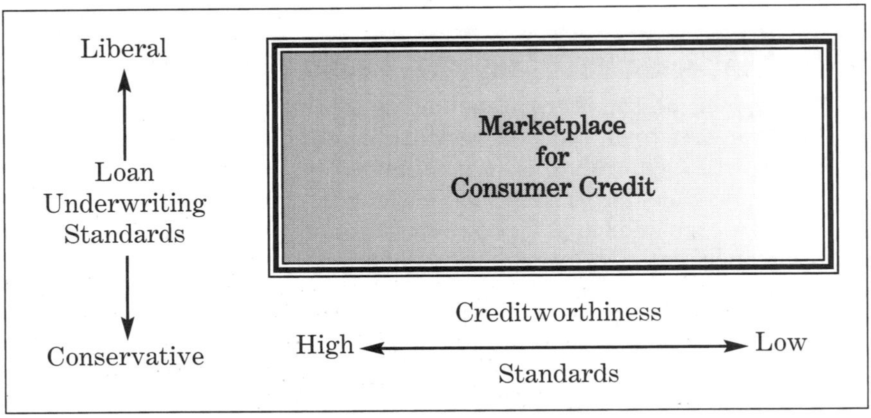

[Diagram: Loan Underwriting Standards (Liberal ↕ Conservative) vs. Creditworthiness Standards (High ← → Low), with "Marketplace for Consumer Credit" filling the chart area.]

Exhibit 2 depicts what might be considered the normal risk group, or applicants most likely to qualify for a loan at a regulated financial institution.

Exhibit 2: Acceptable Risk Group

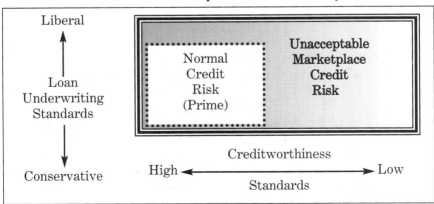

Chapter 1: Prudent Lending Practices and Nonprime Credit Risk

Due-diligence findings and published static pool analysis of both prime and nonprime consumer loan portfolio performance indicate that, regardless of the asset type or risk classification, those that perform as expected have been originated under very similar credit risk management strategies.

Although the relationship differs between the two key components, loan underwriting and creditworthiness standards, the approach to the underlying individual risk components is very similar.

Exhibit 3 depicts the acceptable credit risk categories for prime and nonprime portfolios that have demonstrated favorable performance over time.

Exhibit 3: Prime/Nonprime Creditworthiness Groups

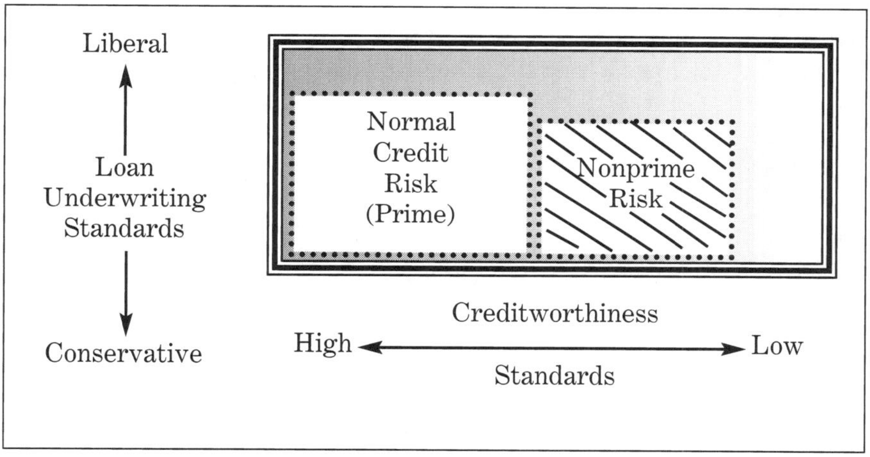

The diagram shows a distinct difference in the risk acceptance relationships for loan underwriting standards and creditworthiness standards between normal (or prime) and nonprime market segments.

In the prime segment, the applicant's demonstrated history of repayment enables the lender to utilize loan underwriting standards commensurate with the probability of orderly loan repayment, over time. When properly interpreted, the down payment, term, rate, and other noncreditworthiness-related underwriting standards (including affordability) are less important and, as such, can be less restrictive. The result is a loan origination program with very favorable loan terms and few, if any, conditions associated with the approval of any one applicant.

Conversely, as the acceptable creditworthiness standards traverse from high to low, the transition from prime to varying degrees of nonprime takes place. As the propensity to not pay on time or pay at all increases, lenders who have successfully remained profitable in this segment have offset the risk by taking a more conservative approach with respect to their loan underwriting standards.

Simply put, they recognize the increased exposure to default cannot be offset entirely by rate alone. Therefore, most successful programs have been driven by strategies such as limiting the amount of the loan (advance), the repayment term, and/or incorporating financial responsibility criteria into the underwriting requirements (e.g., minimum income or other budget constraints).

PITFALLS OF EXPANSION

Very few originators, if any, ever intended to give away the store when entering the nonprime market. However, analysis of a number of entries (particularly failures) indicated it is extremely difficult to limit expansion strictly to the targeted market for two basic reasons: competition for deals and the steadfast unwavering belief of most credit managers that they can profitably buy paper which is outside of the box.

Exhibits 4 and 5 depict the intended penetration and the probable penetration based on historical and ongoing research.

The results of the expansion activities, as diagramed in Exhibit 5, show that although the expansion has occurred with respect to the desired target group, it did not stop there.

Exhibit 4: Intended Penetration

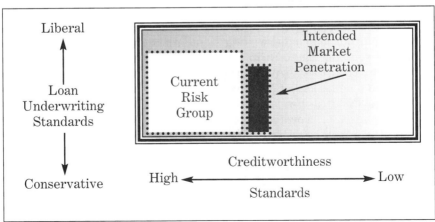

Chapter 1: Prudent Lending Practices and Nonprime Credit Risk

Exhibit 5: Probable Penetration

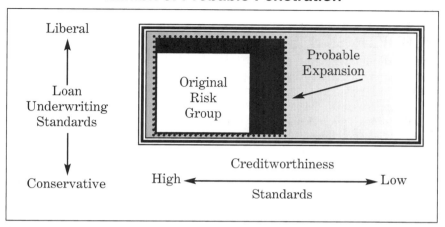

The expansion resulted in the acceptance of some nonprime credit risks associated with the loan underwriting standards reserved only for the original group. In addition, adverse expansion took place with regard to loan underwriting standards within the original risk group, as shown in Exhibit 6.

Exhibit 6: Undesirable Expansion

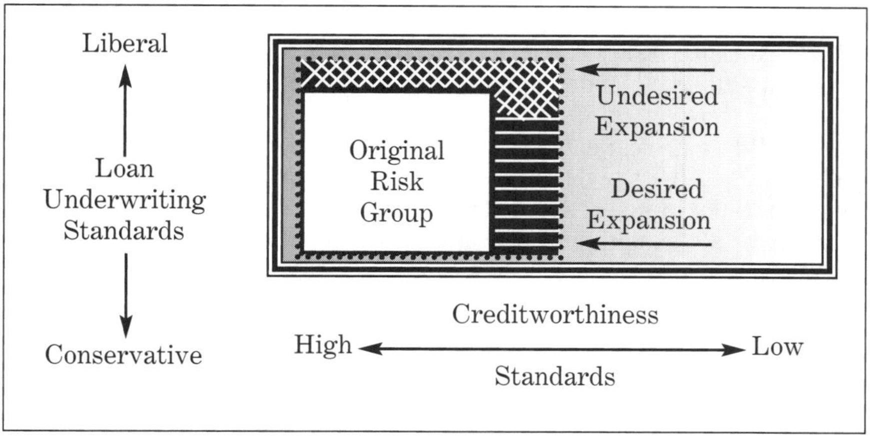

Analysis of this phenomenon supports the theory that the acceptance of credits which have traditionally been unacceptable and/or the natural tendency of credit personnel to buy outside the program (for whatever reason), result in the situation shown in Exhibit 6. This is common to most failed nonprime originators and probably in many nonperforming prime portfolios as well.

CREDIT RISK STRATEGIES

Taking the analysis one step further, an exhaustive review of individual loan underwriting strategies employed by both prime and nonprime consumer lenders (secured and unsecured), supports the premise that a conscious approach to risk management at the underwriting level promotes favorable or expected portfolio performance.

In other words, it is apparent that developing a successful nonprime consumer lending program requires a clear-cut, well defined credit risk management plan — one that transfers the overall profit model assumptions into individual loan origination requirements (utilized in the application approval/rejection process).

When viewed from an implementation perspective, it becomes clear that profitable underwriting programs tend to operate under the premise that:

- The published underwriting program is the rule
- Exceptions or deviations from the rule are limited in both number and type
- Exceptions, when permitted, are subject to critical review by experienced personnel
- All exceptions — regardless of the source or ultimate approval/authorization — are subject to continuous monitoring from the perspective of delinquency and loss severity.

While it has been relatively easy (in the past) to enter the nonprime market, the very nature of the customer and the channel of distribution or point of sale create extremely high barriers to success for long-term survival — depth of the originators pockets notwithstanding.

LOAN ORIGINATION PROGRAMS

Long before the introduction of the application review matrix score or the bureau-driven approve-or-reject scoring models, the decision to approve or reject an application was based on what was commonly referred to as the Five C's: credit, collateral, capacity, character, and conditions.

For purposes of credit risk analysis and the underwriting process, however, the Five C's could be condensed or combined into three categories of risk: deal structure, ability to pay, and, creditworthiness.

Deal Structure

Deal structure concerns issues related to the finance contract and the collateral securing the loan. Interest rate, repayment term, soft adds, minimum/maximum payment, loan amount, advance, down payment, collateral acceptability and use, among other issues, would fall into this category.

Ability to Pay

"If it's raining ... they ain't comin'!" an astute observer of human behavior remarked regarding the probable attendance of his numerous friends at his own funeral. A parallel in the nonprime arena regarding debt-to-income ratios might be, "If they don't have the money ... they don't pay!" (The nonprime borrowers that budget and plan for a rainy day are few and far between.)

The applicant's ability to pay should be based on his or her monthly net income, monthly expenses, and the number of people who live off that figure. Although determining an accurate dollar amount is not always an easy task, it is a necessary one if retail financing, at the lowest possible price to the consumer, is part of the philosophy of the originator.

Given the fact that applicants spend dollars and cents as opposed to percents, reliance on a monthly payment and/or the total debt-to-income ratio makes sense only if the ratios are adjusted downward as the uncertainty of the applicant's surplus or residual income increases.

Creditworthiness

The creditworthiness of the applicant oftentimes is relegated to a review of the credit bureau report, and perhaps not even that if the application is scored as a "pass" or "approved" by an automated scorecard. While this approach may not be all bad in a true environment of 100% accept or reject (based on the scorecard), it happens only rarely in real-life lending — which sets the stage for undesirable credit risk expansion.

This aspect of risk expansion is further compounded by originators who counteract poor performance by making rate adjustments, as opposed to focusing on the fundamentals of the credit extension process for the root cause of the problem.

Creditworthiness, in the "spirit and intent" of prudent lending practices, should focus not only on the data recorded in the credit bureau, but on the applicant's character and stability as well. Character must be included in the analysis, given the fact that the probability of repayment is driven by an historical look back at the applicant's attitude toward financial responsibility. Astute originators require detailed explanations of unfavorable findings to assist in the process without being swayed by other facets of the proposed transaction (such as good dealer or lender-owned [repossessed] collateral being financed).

Stability, although less important, is still a valid component of the creditworthiness review, since residency and employment tenure play a significant role in the ability to maintain financial responsibility over time. The exclusion of character and stability criteria from the overall creditworthiness standards review should be considered a serious deviation from the overall credit risk management process.

CONDITIONS

While it is true that conditions of approval or stipulations are part of the Five C's of credit, research indicates that conditions add value only when used to strengthen a marginal application package rather than to justify an otherwise unacceptable one.

Based on forensics analysis of defaulted and nonperforming automobile-secured sales finance contracts, conditions are really the result of making exceptions to the program that tend to create loss rather than incremental profits. Put another way, approving an application package which does not "pass" the scorecard or "fit" other requirements, simply goes against the intended purpose of the "card" or the underlying underwriting requirements — to control risk.

With the advent of the bureau-driven scorecards and expanded acceptance/usage over the past 10 years or so, very few credit managers have the skills and experience necessary to consistently second-guess the automated decision-making process. The goal of the "human touch" should be to approve more automatic rejects that will pay than rejects that ultimately default — over time.

BREAKING THE RULES

As previously stated, managing the credit risk requires constant monitoring of portfolio development, particularly with regard to exceptions to the underwriting program. Research indicates that when a limited number of exceptions are made to the program and each is offset by a corresponding risk-reduction characteristic (in either the underwriting or creditworthiness standards), incremental profits are possible.

The same research also indicates that when exceptions are made without regard to the impact on risk, deterioration can be expected in the projected delinquency rates, default frequency, and loss severity for the portfolio (on a static pool basis). In other words, when exceptions are not controlled (made without regard to their impact on risk) as they exceed

15% of the loans in the portfolio, significant deterioration in performance can be expected.

A Case in Point

A recent study on the impact of exceptions made during the loan approval process to two automobile portfolios dramatically illustrates the impact of exceptions that are not adequately controlled.

The transactions compared in the case study were nonprime automobile loans, originated on an indirect basis during the same relative time period and under very similar underwriting programs. Both used a scorecard to screen applicants but not as the final word in approval. All approvals were based on a subjective review of the application package and bureau score.

Collections were conducted on a similar basis, as well, which included the use of predictive dialers. The decision to repossess was targeted at 40-50 days delinquent, subject to supervisory review and approval, with third-party repossession agents used to gain custody of the vehicle. All sales of repossessed collateral were facilitated through industry-accepted auction houses.

The results of the study and the impact of granting exceptions thereto are set forth in Exhibit 7 and Exhibit 8.

Exhibit 7: At-Origination Data — Portfolios with Exceptions

	Portfolio A	Portfolio B
Number of loans	1,500	1,502
Average loan amount	$8,400	$8,950
Average repayment terms (months)	44	52
Average gross profit per loan (Paid-out basis)	$1,260	$1,340

Exhibit 8: Underwriting Exceptions Data

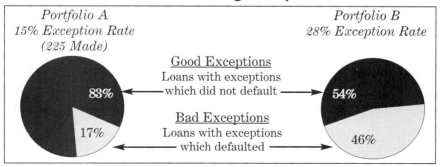

These data presume that, had the loan not been granted an exception to the published criteria, the application would have been withdrawn by the source (typically, a dealership).

Exhibit 9 illustrates the impact exceptions had on profitability for the two portfolios reviewed.

Exhibit 9: Exceptions and Portfolio Profitability

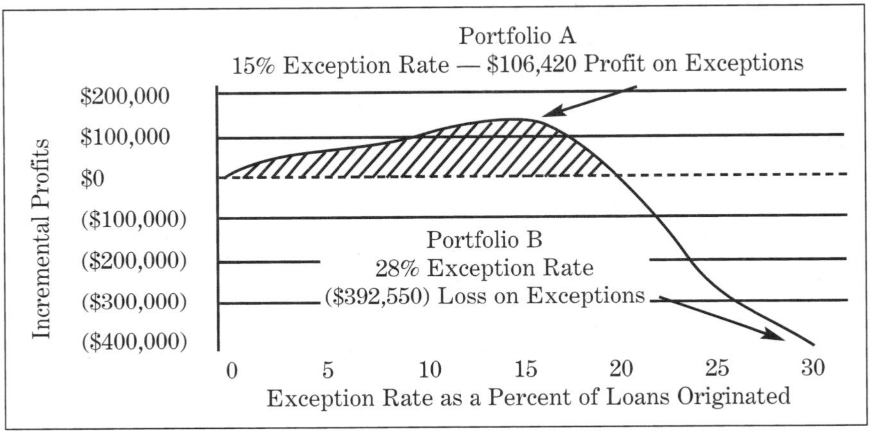

Portfolio A
15% Exception Rate — $106,420 Profit on Exceptions

Portfolio B
28% Exception Rate
($392,550) Loss on Exceptions

Incremental Profits (y-axis): $200,000, $100,000, $0, ($100,000), ($200,000), ($300,000), ($400,000)

Exception Rate as a Percent of Loans Originated (x-axis): 0, 5, 10, 15, 20, 25, 30

Additional analysis was conducted with respect to the individual exceptions to determine if those made for creditworthiness-related issues were more successful than those in the loan-underwriting standards area.

The analysis seems to support the premise that credit managers are slightly more successful when dealing with creditworthiness standards (69% successful versus 62% for loan underwriting standards). However, the overall failure ratio of 35%, coupled with the compounding impact of loss severity (approximately $3,500 in loss versus $1,300 in profit), supports the premise that compliance to underwriting should remain the rule and exceptions granted only when subject to specific risk-reduction criteria standards.

Scott C. Calahan is chairman and president of Boston Portfolio Advisors, Inc. Calahan is responsible for the firm's professional practice and is the majority shareholder in the firm. He has over 20 years of experience in mortgage finance, auto finance, consumer finance, project finance, secondary marketing, and systems development.

He is co-author of *Direct Costing For Life Insurance Company Operations* (published in 1978 by the Life Office Management Association) and was formerly associate editor of the *Journal of Operations Research*.

Calahan is a licensed mortgage broker and has been listed in *Who's Who In Finance and Industry* and *Who's Who In the World*. He is also a frequent speaker for national trade associations and is an outside director of several privately held corporations.

He has directed due-diligence reviews of loan and lease portfolios located in each of the 50 states, Canada, and most European nations. Several of these reviews involved over 10,000 loans and leases each.

He has been a pioneer in the use of operations research and actuarial methodologies to evaluate mortgage loan and auto loan portfolio performance. The results of the work have been used for cash-flow forecasting, loss prevention, loss reserve adequacy analysis, risk-based pricing, prepayment analysis, and strategic planning.

His education includes a bachelor of science degree in finance from Pennsylvania State University, a master's degree in business administration from the University of Pittsburgh (Ford Foundation fellowship), and Ph.D. studies in operations research at Case Western Reserve University.

Chapter 2

Risk-Based Pricing

Scott C. Calahan
Chairman and President
Boston Portfolio Advisors

Risk-based pricing, at its simplest, is a framework for measuring and predicting risk, then adjusting prices to produce the desired target returns. This chapter will discuss a framework of concepts that Boston Portfolio Advisors has found work consistently well — along with some concepts that often *do not* work very well.

What do we want to accomplish by means of risk-based pricing? First, we want to determine which risks are important. All sorts of risks become apparent in the study of subprime lending: Some are important at certain points in a product cycle, some are important with some products but not with others.

The measurement of historic risk is interesting and useful; but, even more important, we want to estimate future risk. As the old wag said, all of our knowledge is about the past and all of our decisions are about the future. So, while we can study to death the past, it may or may not look like the future. If the past has been "ugly," we want to develop pricing and product strategies that induce change and result in superior performance.

We want to identify structural components of price. The most common structural components that can be included in the original loan, lease, or sales finance contract include:

- Interest rate and rules for change.
- Discounts and points.
- Teaser rates and terms.
- Exceptions policy.
- Other rules governing when and how payments are to be made.

The most common financial components of price include loan losses and dilution, operating expenses, capital costs, and profit margin.

Many subprime markets are not dominated by vertically integrated organizations. Instead, most subprime credit markets have decentralized delivery and aggregation systems.

Each participant along the way, from originator to final securitization investor, has limited ability to impose or change the pricing rules of the marketplace. As a result, participants seek to divert any available piece of the cash flows from the borrower or obligor. All cash-flow diversion decisions along the way are really risk-based pricing decisions. Organizations that are successful make highly creative pricing decisions to capture more cash flow than risk. Many diversion strategies are highly proprietary, and any discussion in this chapter of these proprietary structures is generic for purposes of demonstration only.

The lower limit to each of the individual pricing decisions is typically the expected cost plus required margin (however calculated). The upper limit is the price quote of an alternate investor or function substitute (for example, retail instead of wholesale loan production, B piece investor, risk default insurer, or risk retention). A participant can participate within these limits or can elect not to participate; not participating reduces the ultimate size of the product market.

WHOSE RISK ARE WE MEASURING?

Different groups and individuals in a financial product origination/servicing/collections cycle have different roles and perspectives, with a variety of risks and needs. If all of those variables aren't addressed or cared for, we often do not achieve the intended results.

Obviously, the people who provide capital deserve a shot at getting the kind of portfolio performance returns they want for the risk they are taking. If their principal dollars go away in large measure, if their yields are not what they expected, they tend to become angry; they remove their capital and allocate it elsewhere.

Servicers are at risk if delinquency and default rates are higher than expected, if costs are higher. They are also at risk if prepayments are drastically higher than predicted, resulting in lower revenues than expected.

Originators will generate little volume and revenue if the pricing and product features are not competitive. Sometimes we have the most wonderful model but get no volume.

Aggregators who collect the loans and leases have a right to expect only a limited amount of fraud, reasonable volumes, and a portfolio that can be sold or securitized at a profit.

Borrowers and obligors have to find the product affordable and attractive. If the product is to survive and flourish, its features, pricing, and performance have to work for everybody in the "food chain." It should not be surprising that, in the world of subprime consumer lending, most new products fail.

We want to implement management reporting and surveillance systems. Far too often, a product's structure and pricing is set and it is launched into the marketplace only to find, six months or a year later, that the result has been the acquisition of a tremendous volume of ill-conceived assets. The objective of management reporting and surveillance is to achieve superior portfolio performance. The sooner we know our portfolio is off track, the sooner we can implement corrections and the better the ultimate portfolio performance will become.

WHICH RISKS ARE IMPORTANT?

Risks that are critically important vary by industry. The make-or-break performance benchmarks vary from category to category among subprime industries. The subprime mortgage banking and home equity industries, for example, have been shattered recently with high prepayments; as a result, cash flows have ground to a halt. High costs of origination, and premium purchase prices, have been rewarded with a very short average loan life and reduced revenue. Defaults, while important, have had a much less dramatic impact.

The subprime auto finance business, in contrast, has been decimated with fraud, high default rates, high loss severity, and high loan losses since the mid-1990s. Prepayments, in contrast, have been only a minor problem as they are infrequent. Finance companies typically purchase loans at a discount, from dealers. When a subprime auto prepayment occurs, it usually generates a realized gain.

Risks vary greatly by credit grade as well as by company. A variety of origination structures and marketing platforms are used and, as a consequence, not all companies will have the same exposure and needs.

Risks change over time. What is important this year may not be quite as important next year or in the total life of the product cycle.

The 'D' Words

Many subprime risks that came to the forefront in the late 1990s can be summed up in words beginning with the letter D:

Delinquency Slows down cash flow, increases collection costs, and leads to defaults.

Default Frequency and Timing The leading risk in most subprime products. Of every hundred loans or leases, how many will have a terminal default — no more borrower payments — throughout the life of the pool?

Default Timing While the frequency of defaults is critical, so is the timing. If we have a portfolio of 360-month mortgage loans and 100 out of 100 default — but all default in month 360 — the overall pool cash-flow performance would still be excellent. However, if they all default in the first month, the pool cash-flow performance would be disastrous. The timing of defaults affects cash flow in several ways, including number of regular payments received and recoveries from repossession, foreclosure, or litigation.

Loss Severity When a default occurs, how much of the principal dollar is lost? Severity is usually measured as a the ratio of principal dollars lost (after collateral recoveries) to the current principal balance or, alternately, to the original principal balance. Factors that influence loss severity include loan-to-value ratio, the timing of defaults, and whether the collateral asset is appreciating or depreciating. If a loan or lease defaults, do we lose 10% of the principal, 50%, or everything? A portfolio can have high defaults and low severity — producing acceptable losses. Conversely, a portfolio with low defaults and high severity can produce equivalent losses. It is the portfolio with high defaults and high severity that produces disastrous losses.

Dilution Generally defined as loss of cash flow due to causes other than borrower default. In prime-quality and subprime trade receivables, for example, dilution routinely occurs as a result of discounts and rebates. Subprime mortgage bankers often suffer dilution when they buy loans at a premium, assuming a long average life, then experience rapid prepayments. This risk is most visible with the gain-on-sale accounting reversals that have decimated the balance sheets and financial viability of some companies. While these examples are easy to understand, dilution is often more subtle in the subprime auto loan markets. Dilution can occur for reasons as simple as granting a payment extension to a delinquent borrower. Or it can occur for subtle reasons often disguised by internal staff complicit in its occurrence. Most servicing systems are not capable of measuring dilution, leaving a portfolio manager with not only dilution risk but also measurement risk.

Duration The risk that actual timing of cash-flow receipts will not match expected timing, defined as duration, is a critical consideration for some investors. Rapid subprime mortgage prepayments on senior securitized certificates may return all of an investor's principal — but much earlier than expected or wanted. The investor may, in turn, have matched the expected average asset life and duration to a liability or other obligation.

Capital Adequacy Not a D word, but important all the same. It is essential to determine what capital level is necessary to support the aggregate portfolio risk, then to assess the risk that this level of capital will be inadequate. This is a topic of considerable academic and actuarial discussion, loosely summarized as the study of the risks of individual portfolios and the degree to which these risks are correlated in the aggregate. To the extent that they are not correlated, a lesser capital base can support all underlying portfolios. To the extent that they are highly correlated, more capital is needed. Subprime financial organizations that are part of larger entities can view capital adequacy in this context. However, many subprime financial organizations are independent, single-product entities without a lifeline from a parent company of additional capital if needed in time of distress. For them, the capital adequacy risk is simply the risk of survival.

Survival Our final risk is, simply, survival. Incorrect product pricing, incorrect product structure, and inattention to risk have killed companies.

MEASURING RISK

Now that we have identified a number of risks that need our consideration, how do we begin to measure them? The place to start is, obviously, getting data — curiously enough, usually the most difficult part of the process. In some new-product situations there may not be any historic data. When considering major product changes, historic data may not be a very good guide to future performance.

Data Banks

But one has to start somewhere — generally, with whatever data are available, in whatever form. This can include information from internal records, suppliers, investors, consultants, rating agencies, internet web sites — whatever you can get your hands on. Competitor securitization performance data are often available.

Get everything you can think of that might possibly be useful, for as many historic periods as possible. If you can get three *months* worth of data, that is great; if you can get three *years* — that is better. More than that is terrific. Between changes and conversions of servicing systems and changes in products, though, you have to be careful about what you get and how you use it. Try to find performance data that can give insight to the risks you believe are important. Be careful not to violate data export restrictions from other countries. Create a static pool analysis. This is a core technique for measuring risks, cash flows, and income realities. The results can be used to take a serious measure of risk-based pricing opportunities.

A PRIMER ON STATIC POOL ANALYSIS

The default-rate and loss-rate intensity of most subprime loan and lease products vary widely by their age or seasoning. Default rates start low, rise for some months, peak, and begin to fall. The deeper the credit, the more intense the shape of the curve. This pattern is present in most credit portfolios. In subprime portfolios where these patterns are pronounced, measuring average default rates by using segments with varying age times produces erroneous results. Growing portfolios mask loss intensity. Static pool analysis is a methodology that isolates a group of loans originated in the same time period, then measures their performance each month or quarter. There is a useful and fundamental principle that can be used in static pool analyses:

Frequency of loss × severity of loss = portfolio losses.

Frequency is simply the percentage of loans that will default over the life of the pool. Severity is how much we are going to lose. Severity can be measured as a percentage of original loan principal balance or as a percentage of current balance at the time of default. Both measures are useful. One approach will be much more useful than another depending on the portfolios. Simple regression analyses can help determine which will be better, and it is useful to have both.

A word of caution: In measuring loss severity, be certain the accounting is consistent; attempt to make it as close as possible to industry gain-on-sale accounting practices.

Begin by "eyeballing" — studying — the data. Use more advanced methods to merge data of static pools and terminal events, if — and only if — they are similar. If dissimilar kinds of pools are merged, the analysis can reach conclusions that are not valid.

Any risk can be measured by static pool analysis, although defaults and prepayments are the two most commonly tracked. Exhibit 1 shows typical quarterly default rate patterns for B-grade and D-grade subprime auto loan portfolios.

Exhibit 1: B and D Grade Quarterly Default Rates

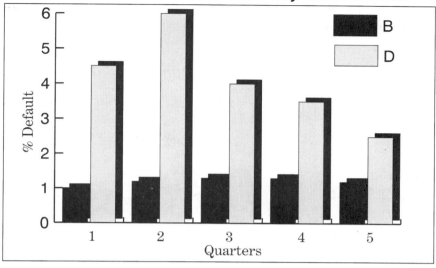

Both start low, rise, peak, and begin falling. The D-grade default rate is not only higher than the B-grade default rate, but also occurs earlier. The result is higher defaults and losses, and lower regular cash flow before defaults occur. Exhibit 2 shows the same data on a cumulative basis. It is useful to track data both on a period and a cumulative basis.

Exhibit 2: B and D Grade Cumulative Default Rates

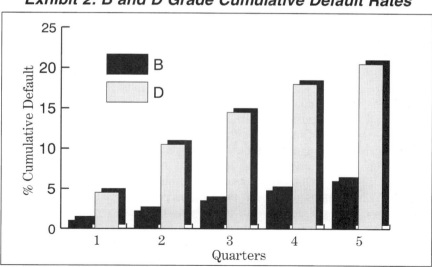

There are many reporting formats used to display static pool analysis results. Several are shown here. Exhibit 3, a triangular layout, shows cumulative results for each month of experience and each month of origination.

Exhibit 3: Sample D Grade Cumulative Defaults

Origination Volume ($ Millions)	1	Month of Origination 2	3	4	5
	1.214	2.638	3.492	4.116	4.771

Number of Payments Before Default	1	Month of Origination 2	3	4	5
0	1.25	1.31	1.34	1.27	1.21
1	1.60	1.63	1.66	1.45	1.41
2	1.50	1.53	1.56	1.48	
3	1.64	1.61	1.64		
4	1.55	1.60			
5	1.47				

Use separate formats to show delinquency, defaults, losses, and other risks. The advantage of these formats is that they is easy to understand and not difficult to generate once loan level performance data are in the proper form. The disadvantage of the formats is that they cannot easily merge the experience of a group of months. Merging the experience can be important with rapidly growing portfolios where the newer months have the greatest volume but also the least cumulative experience.

Boston Portfolio Advisors has developed proprietary computer systems to merge the experience of a number of months. By merging the experience, a baseline curve can be developed showing as many risks as useful, and their interaction, although the focus is typically on defaults, loss severity, losses, and prepayments. Any number of months can be safely merged as long as the monthly portfolios are "homogeneous" — no major changes in underwriting guidelines, pricing, competitive conditions, or the like. Exhibit 4 shows a simple auto loan portfolio.

This baseline curve can be used directly to measure cash flows, timing, and time effects, and, ultimately, to evaluate revenue adequacy. The interaction between defaults and prepayments is not significant with this hypothetical auto loan portfolio, but note that these interactions can be significant in other portfolios.

Exhibit 4: Sample Auto Loan Portfolio Loss And Prepayment Development Curve

Months Seasoning	Monthly % Default	Cumulative % Default	Cumulative Defaults as % of Lifetime	Monthly Loss %	Cumulative % Losses	Cumulative Losses as % of Lifetime	Monthly Prepayment %	Cumulative Prepayment %	Cumulative Prepayments as % of Lifetime
0	1.250%	1.250%	2.8%	0.594%	0.594%	3.96%	0.000%	0.000%	0.00%
1	1.500	2.750	6.1	0.705	1.299	8.66	0.005	0.005	0.03
2	1.500	4.250	9.4	0.696	1.995	13.30	0.007	0.012	0.05
3	1.640	5.890	13.1	0.751	2.746	18.31	0.021	0.033	0.14
4	1.550	7.440	16.5	0.701	3.446	22.98	0.025	0.058	0.17
5	1.470	8.910	19.8	0.657	4.104	27.36	0.031	0.089	0.21

THE BEGINNING OF UNDERSTANDING

By evaluating static pool analysis results, we begin to see which risks are important and which are not, where losses occur and where they do not. In a subprime auto portfolio, defaults often differ by credit grade, credit score range, debt-to-income ratio range, geographic territory, dealer group, and by dealer. Subprime mortgage loans have similar patterns.

A grasp of magnitudes and timing patterns can show, in simple terms, what is important and what is not. They can give you a feel for which items need to be addressed explicitly, or whether you can say, "We looked at it and that was that."

More advanced statistical models can be powerful, but these models become extremely complex to use properly, particularly when running multivariate analyses with time series. Attempting to create a scorecard or a similar structure will usually bump into the limits of the statistical routines themselves. Such exercises are best left in the hands of skilled, experienced professionals who understand the uses and limits of parametric and nonparametric statistics.

Boston Portfolio Advisors' general experience with these methodologies has been that unless you have extremely good data and lots of time available, many of these models may be interesting as topics of conversation but don't serve much of a practical purpose. You have only 10 days to prepare your bid for a portfolio — and it will take four months to assemble the necessary data — you are more than three and a half months shy of being competitive.

Historic Data

Some limits on historic data are worth mentioning. One is that typically these data are limited. We may have only a few time periods, incomplete or inaccessible data, or data locked in systems that are inaccessible (mainframes). Without a major programming effort it will be very difficult to retrieve data. Often, a useful approach over time is to create a stand-alone relational data base, importing data from all available sources that can be "mined."

Many circumstances render existing data nearly useless. With a new product introduction, for example, there may be no historic data. Competitive changes — whether your own or your competitor's, can reduce the usefulness and relevance of historic data.

Change in economic conditions is a factor many people worry about the most. Boston Portfolio Advisors' experiences have often shown that many subprime borrowers are already in their own personal recession, and that macroeconomic deterioration may not give as much personal woe to them as it does to prime borrowers.

Lookalikes If we don't have historic data, what can we do? Sometimes, "lookalike" product data are available. The lookalike source might be your own experience. But other products serving the same product market may not be identical to the product in question. Often, competitor data are available, which can be extremely useful. Determine whether you would be satisfied with their results if they were your own. Third-party data, particularly credit scores, can be useful if available. We have found third-party borrower income estimates can be very useful, particularly for deep credit subprime auto borrowers, low DOC/no DOC subprime mortgage borrowers, and nonprime equipment lease obligors.

Abuse In the case of subprime auto loans, a considerable percentage of the reported data has been falsified by the dealers and the borrowers. Mortgage loan low-documentation, stated-income, and no-documentation formats invite mortgage broker and borrower abuse in the subprime markets. Nonprime equipment lease obligor income is often not reported due to industry competitive practices. Because the performance of most subprime portfolios is sensitive to both income levels and debt-to-income ratios, any amount of income data beyond none at all can be a powerful aid to risk analysis and control.

Boston Portfolio Advisors' experience is that market research can be particularly effective in understanding why retail originators (whether auto dealers, mortgage brokers, lease brokers, or the like) will favor one competitor over another with a piece of business. Determine all you can about competitor's practices and pricing structures. Computer simulation modeling is another approach to the exploration of risk impact when data are not readily available. By varying assumptions within probable ranges, one at a time and in combinations, you can often develop insights about risks that are sometimes crucial, sometimes irrelevant.

Product Testing There is nothing quite as illuminating as finding out if your great invention will work, if it will produce the results you want and be competitive. If your sales force and distributors actually sell it, will your warehouse lenders and investors provide capital?

BEGINNING THE PROCESS

Having completed these steps, how does one start to close the circle and begin the product pricing process? A useful first step is to determine one or more break-even pricing scenarios — the lowest combinations of rates, discounts, and terms which could be charged and break even. At the same time, determine the highest which could be charged before your product would become noncompetitive. If you find that this "noncompetitive break-even" price is lower than the lowest financial beak-even price, kill the product or redesign it. If the margins are inadequate, do the same.

If the margins appear adequate, refine the cash flow models, test, and retest. Test them for market share, volumes, default and prepayment rates, loss severities, timing distributions, costs, and capital charges. Test combinations of risks, prices, outcomes, and returns. Perform stress testing and evaluate the results. When successfully evaluated combinations are found that do not have disastrous stress-testing results, a successful test marketing product is in the offing.

Here are a few additional considerations:

- Does your set of pricing or pricing structures work for everybody in the "food chain?" If it doesn't work, think carefully about going forward. Think about the impact on market share and competitive retaliation. If it appears to be hugely profitable, it may not be competitive. Think about the opposite possibility: If a product is ultracompetitive the reward is sometimes a huge market share with more volume than can be processed effectively, resulting in the penalty of ugly losses and cash flows. Somewhere in between is likely to be a highly rewarding balance.

- Will the capital markets accept it? Can you get equity, warehouse, and securitization funds to finance the product?
- What is the cost of incorrect assumptions? If you — or the markets — are wrong, or go wrong, will it hurt you? Can you survive, or will it put you under?

It is crucial to have a plan with assumptions and contingencies. It is equally important to manage those assumptions. It is imperative to control risk after the close of a pool, loan, or lease. So track performance, store as much data in a product performance database as feasible, and evaluate results.

Think about how to be a positive influence on the results. For example, sales forces are usually rewarded for volume. Perhaps they should be rewarded for risk performance and paid for profitability as opposed to just volume for volume's sake. Track results by originator or distribution channel; provide consistent feedback; terminate relations with the worst performers. Install an antifraud program. Not having fraud protection in any of the subprime markets is inviting disaster.

Every originator installs penalties for poor borrower performance. Another and more positive approach can be to install incentives for good borrower behavior. Seek to retain good borrowers rather than force them to do business with your competitor.

Performance Indicators

Here are some easy-to-implement performance indicators:

- First-payment default rate. This is the earliest of the indicators, an excellent clue to fraud level and underwriting effectiveness.
- Early-payment default rate, usually the first three or four months of performance. This is a slightly more mature level of underwriting effectiveness and a good early indicator of lifetime default rate levels.
- Projected life of pool default rate, updated monthly with actual defaults to date plus projected defaults.
- Loss severity.
- Collection rate. Cumulative actual cash flow by month compared with the cost of the assets.
- Delinquency aging.
- Delinquency roll rates. The roll rates measure the percentage of loans or leases moving from one aging category to another in the following month. These data can be very useful is identifying

when collector effectiveness declines and in showing which delinquency stage deserves the most attention.
- Prepayment rate.
- Underwriting exception rates.
- Extension/modification/rewrite rates. Understand how much delinquency is being buried from view.

If your company has any subpar operations, shore them up. If there is weakness in collection, underwriting, sales, or the customer service group, strengthen them. Any of these weaknesses can degrade performance. It is surprising where performance leaks can and do occur.

SUMMARY
As a recap:

- Find sources of data; go wherever needed.
- Determine the major risks, model the cash flows. Understand the likely and severe-case impact on your capital. Even if your approach, it is worth the effort.
- Develop methods to accumulate analyze data.
- Test your product and pricing.
- Monitor your performance.

Really do expect surprises. Some, but not all of them, will be good, and some will be bad. With careful and consistent monitoring you will know when your actual risks are varying from your assumptions.

When you do find risk, don't be afraid to react and to adjust. The consequences of *not* making these adjustments can be severe.

Daniel H. Relf is executive vice president, national loan servicing, for Aames Financial Corporation, which he joined in July 1995.

Prior to his position with Aames, Relf had retired from Great Western Bank where he spent 24 years, serving as senior vice president and director of mortgage servicing since 1986.

During his 34-year career in the financial services industry, Relf has served as a member and past chairman of the California League of Financial Institutions' loan service managers committee. He has also been a member and past president of the Loan Service Managers Association of Southern California.

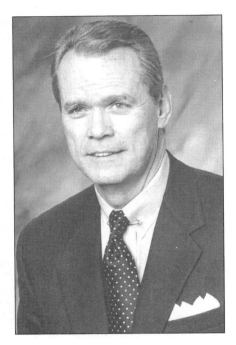

Chapter 3

Subprime Collection Methodology

Daniel H. Relf
Executive Vice President
Aames Financial Corporation

The very nature of the term subprime suggests that such loan portfolios differ in respect to prime portfolios. And on an overall basis they most certainly do. The subprime portfolio consists of loans with differing degrees of credit blemish — from the occasional late payment on unsecured consumer credit to the severest of credit problems, including borrowers in bankruptcy and those whose loans have been placed in foreclosure. In fact, some subprime portfolio business is generated from the refinancing of another lender's defaulted loan just before the scheduled public auction of the underlying collateral on the courthouse steps. A prime portfolio lender would never consider such business – at least not knowingly. Yet even prime portfolios contain a certain segment of loans that are regarded as chronic or, at least, recurring, delinquents. These loans have developed over time the same type of credit characteristics displayed by the loans in a subprime portfolio. The only difference is that they did not start out as subprime.

With this understanding, it can be said that every loan portfolio – no matter how it is characterized — has a subprime component. It may constitute the entire portfolio or some smaller portion; but it exists nevertheless, and represents a formidable challenge to all mortgage loan servicers.

JUST WHO IS THIS BORROWER?

Before undertaking a discussion of effective subprime collection methodology, we need to understand the nature of this delinquent borrower. Statistically speaking, he is characterized by the rating agency, Fitch IBCA, as being in his early forties. He has lived in his mortgaged property for less than two years and has also been on his present job for less than two years. His average annual household income is approximately $36,000.

Of course, this knowledge does not really give us much in the way of meaningful insight into who this borrower really is. For this, we must delve much deeper into what makes up his behavioral pattern.

He Is Prone to Manipulation
One of the most significant factors contributing to this borrower's credit problems is his susceptibility to marketing influences. Such influences are all around us, and we are bombarded by them from every imaginable source. Billions of dollars are spent each year persuading us that a particular brand of automobile will solve many of our problems and enrich our quality of life. A home entertainment center or pleasure watercraft will somehow bring our family closer together. And an exotic vacation — well, just because we deserve it.

Although we all are exposed to these suggestive messages, most of us will not succumb to them to the extent that they become deleterious to our financial health. Unfortunately, the subprime borrower all too often is not so immune, instant gratification being the downfall of this individual.

There Is No Dearth of Accomplices
He cannot find himself in this predicament, however, without being aided and abetted by a plethora of prospective creditors. As he attempts to gratify his insatiable desires, these creditors seem all too willing to extend to him the credit that is necessary. The idea of saving for a particular goal, or the joy of anticipation is just not within this borrower's realm of experience.

WHAT IS THIS BORROWER'S FRAME OF REFERENCE?
This borrower is not new to the collection process practiced by his prior or current creditors. And depending upon how far he has fallen from grace in his credit activities, he has experienced all manner of efforts to get his attention and persuade him, or compel him, as the case may be, to bow to the wishes and desires of his cadre of creditors.

One might say that he knows the tricks of the trade every bit as well or better than the creditor who is hounding him. He has heard all the approaches and, thus far, survived all the efforts to compel compliance. After all, he is still in the property and a member of the fraternity that counts among its accomplishments homeownership, which is, of course, the American dream.

In a number of respects, he is more familiar with the legal enforcement processes than are the collection staff members representing his creditors. He has lived these processes and consequently has firsthand experience with the arcane avenues associated with lien perfection and obligation enforcement. On the other hand, creditors' representatives usually have no more than a theoretical and cursory understanding of the process, putting them at a distinct disadvantage — at least where tactical issues are concerned.

WHAT KIND OF BEHAVIOR CAN BE EXPECTED FROM THIS BORROWER?

First of all, there are myriad reasons why this type of borrower is in his current predicament. They range from income curtailment to unexpected expenses to personal tragedy.

A number of years ago, there was a television drama series called Naked City. In the prologue each week, the off-camera announcer always would begin by saying, "There are eight million stories in the naked city — this is just one of them." Similarly, each defaulting subprime borrower has his own story, and no two are exactly alike. But a common theme runs through most of them. The blame for the problem is placed upon some outside influence or exogenous force. The borrower does not take responsibility for his situation; he is the victim, and nobody is going to convince him otherwise. The slightest suggestion of any personal responsibility will be met with nothing short of utter indignation.

Is It Apathy or a Lack of Anxiety?

A common reaction of many creditors' representatives is that the borrower does not seem to care; the common parlance used among creditors and collectors is that the borrower has an "improper regard for the obligation." So creditors' representatives just shake their heads in bewilderment, since they cannot comprehend how somebody could be teetering on the brink of losing his home and not be expressing concern over it. But there is a difference between apathy and lack of anxiety.

Almost no subprime borrower is apathetic about the prospect that he may lose his home through foreclosure. He cares as much as anybody would — this is not what his apparent lack of concern is really manifesting. Instead, in an effort to retain his sanity and some semblance of normalcy in his life, he has developed a heightened ability to compartmentalize his problems. In this way, he can park his problems on the sidelines of life, giving him a way not to cope but to coexist with his problems. To understand this dynamic is to take the first major step in dealing effectively with the subprime borrower.

WHAT IS IT THAT WE WANT TO ACCOMPLISH?

To attempt the charting of a course before we know where we want it to take us is to wander aimlessly, not knowing where or when our journey will end. So we must first decide what it is that we want to achieve.

In some circles, emphasis is placed on the quantity of cash that can be brought in the door each month; so if a monthly installment can be coaxed out of a borrower when several are past due, this is regarded as a successful result. The fact that communication with this borrower next month is necessitated by this strategy seems to matter not. Certainly, the account has not suffered further deterioration, but there is no improvement to celebrate either. It is like a swimmer caught in a riptide — not yet drowned but, yet, no closer to shore. He treads water while his energy continues to dissipate.

And what of the costs that this approach creates? Rather than establishing an environment in which this borrower eventually can rise out of the muck that has him so bemired, he is destined to remain entrapped as a perpetual burden on the cost structure of the collection enterprise. Encouraging such behavior is a short-sighted strategy that has no long-term benefits for either the borrower or the creditor.

A more enlightened approach is one that has as its goal the rehabilitation of the borrower, with the consequential benefits it has for him as well as the creditor. Remediation affords the borrower opportunities to repair his credit and reduce the expense associated with credit. In the world of the subprime borrower, a year's worth of timely mortgage payments can create the ability to replace the existing mortgage with one carrying a significantly lower interest rate and correspondingly smaller monthly installments.

It is interesting to note that in so many situations the status achieved after realization of a specific goal can be very difficult to maintain, whereas the opportunities unfolding for this borrower after remediation become ever more easily accomplished.

The creditor reaps substantial benefits as well. Successful efforts at rehabilitating the borrower produce more consistent cash flows while at the same time lowering expenses. The operation runs more efficiently through greater leveraging of available resources. It is a mutually beneficial result where everybody occupies the winner's circle. And it can be done, but not just because we will it so.

THE OBVIOUS APPROACH TO ANYTHING IS ALL TOO OFTEN WRONG

When we take a look at the typical mortgage document, the "rule book" describing the relationship between the borrower and the creditor, it is abundantly clear that the creditor is holding all of the cards. For just about any indiscretion the borrower might commit, there is a consequence in favor of the creditor; the ultimate price being the fact that the creditor can evict the borrower from his home and sell it out from under him.

It should be obvious, then, that what the creditor says goes. After all, anybody in his right mind should be willing to do whatever it takes to keep from losing his home. So it shouldn't matter much how a creditor's representative demands performance; the fact that he has the necessary power should be all that is important. Just think of the other golden rule: the one with all the gold makes all the rules.

If a borrower dared to violate the "rules," a sharp warning surely would get him back on track and cause him to think twice about ever being so foolish in the future. But, then, if it were this easy, there would be no need for collectors or collection departments. The requisite warning letters could be merely spit out of some computer, and the inconvenience would be hardly noticed.

So why doesn't this approach work? It seems to make sense, if for no other reason than the home mortgage debt is the single most important obligation the consumer has. Without his home, he has no driveway for the new car or boat; no living room to accommodate the entertainment center; no place at all for the new furniture.

The reason this approach doesn't work is not because it doesn't make sense; it doesn't work because the borrower is not approaching the situation from an intellectual point of view. His perspective is purely emotional in nature. He is guided by his feelings — not by rational thought.

If we employ the dictatorial approach in our collection effort because we know we have both the power and authority, it will be met with resentment on the part of the borrower. He will react in a negative way, either by shutting down any two-way communication we are attempting to establish or by stubbornly refusing to cooperate in the effort to resolve the delinquent condition. The dictatorial or autocratic approach merely reminds him of how uncomfortably helpless he feels in his predicament. Pain of any kind, whether physical or emotional, is unpalatable; and we will attempt to avoid it at almost any cost — even when such avoidance has the potential of causing even greater pain in the future!

This is a difficult concept to grasp for many collection operations because it requires either a considerable amount of empathy for, or clinical understanding of, the borrower's state of mind. Just how difficult this concept is to grasp becomes clearer as we consider how different the borrower's frame of reference is from that of the creditor.

As can be seen, the borrower is concentrating his energy on pain avoidance at the emotional level, with any resolution of corporeal issues being purely coincidental in nature. It could be said that he is in survival mode at the most basic level. The natural desire to maintain one's sanity is indeed more powerful than the desire to maintain any material possession.

The creditor's representative, on the other hand, views the situation from a completely pragmatic perspective, void of emotion. The account may be not much more than an identification number with a specific amount past due. Moreover, it is probably only one of hundreds in the collector's daily work queue.

With a few keystrokes, a computer screen fills with cold statistical data about the account. No real suggestion of human drama appears to exist, only numbers and codes that attempt in a feeble way to describe and categorize the borrower and his plight.

Given these dichotomous points of view, there is little wonder the creditor's representative and the borrower are so often not communicating — or at least not communicating effectively. And if they are not communicating effectively, the creditor is squandering resources and may even be alienating the borrower.

Emotions and rational thought are oftentimes incompatable. But if we have any hope of developing effective collection techniques, we must find a way for the two to reach simultaneity. Otherwise, we will not be able to realize the leveraging of resources required if we are to be truly successful in efforts to manage assets effectively.

Human nature is like a natural law; it cannot be disregarded or altered. Any procedure or strategy that does not acknowledge human nature as a constant is destined to be ineffective, if it works at all. And so any successful collection strategy must be conceived with an eye fixed on the intransigent power of human nature.

EXPECT EVERY LOAN TO PERFORM, BUT PLAN FOR ANY LOAN TO FAIL

Effective collection efforts do not start when an account becomes past due, they start as soon as the loan is created and placed into service. With the understanding that a delinquent borrower's frame of reference is emotional in nature, it is important to understand how he feels about his relationship with his creditor. There are specific reasons for this.

For one thing, if he has a positive reaction toward his creditor, he is more likely to be willing to involve himself in open communication. In fact, he may even initiate the first contact. What also needs to be kept in mind is that there will be a number of creditors competing for the available resources of the borrower. In all likelihood, he will be able to pay some creditors but not all of them. Those creditors with whom he has some affinity will have a better chance of getting his attention than those about whom he feels neutral or even some degree of alienation.

TENDENCY TO LIVE UP TO EXPECTATIONS

The first step in the effective collection (or, more generally, the loss mitigation) process is what may be described as the "welcome call." The welcome call is the first opportunity from a servicing point of view to establish the basis for a friendly relationship and the feeling that the creditor genuinely cares about the borrower and his business. This is a great way to get off on the right foot because, quite frankly, in most business relationships once the bargain has been struck the "honeymoon" seems to end abruptly. Just ask yourself how many experiences you can recount in which service matched or exceeded the atmosphere created while you were still in the "buying" mode. In those cases you can recount, didn't you feel exceptionally good about the overall relationship? And wasn't part of your good feeling due to the element of surprise, since you weren't really expecting such quality treatment? So this becomes an opportunity to be set apart from the competition — the competition that will be seeking those same dollars if and when this borrower falls behind in his obligations.

Another purpose of the welcome call is more subliminal in nature. There is a tendency on the part of many consumers in this day and age to feel that they are nothing more than obscure strings of numbers in a massive computer data bank. This tends to produce a feeling of anonymity that can work to the disadvantage of the creditor. It is very much like the contrast between the level of citizenship reflected in a vast metropolis and that in a small town. In the large city, the cloak of anonymity permits us to feel less uncomfortable in exposing the seamier side of our character. In a small town, however, we know we could not get away with such a demeanor because, directly or indirectly, everybody knows one another. The welcome call, then, helps to create more of the atmosphere of the small town by introducing human contact and eliminating the feeling of anonymity. The contact also sets up, in a friendly way, certain expectations on the part of the creditor that will stay with the borrower if, in the ensuing relationship, no resentment is created.

LOSS MITIGATION STARTS WITH EXCEPTIONAL CUSTOMER SERVICE

Although the welcome call is the first servicing opportunity to establish rapport with the borrower, if we were to stop here we would not have achieved our objective. Every opportunity to interact with the borrower gives the creditor an additional chance to demonstrate how important the borrower is. Whether the interaction has anything to do with contract enforcement, or simply customer service in general, the level of service provided will foretell the degree of effectiveness of subsequent collection efforts. And it isn't just good customer service that will serve our purpose; it is exceptional customer service that we must be prepared to provide if we are to achieve our ultimate objective of effective collection practices.

When customer service levels are considered, we must bear in mind what the borrower is expecting. If we provide a timely and accurate response to his inquiry, we have met his expectations. But is this enough? By meeting his expectations, there is certainly nothing to complain about, but neither does it engender any other reaction or feelings. In fact, completely adequate customer service causes nothing more than a neutral feeling on the part of the borrower about the service level rendered. There is nothing memorable about the experience. A request has been made, a response has been provided, and that's that.

For the experience to be memorable, the level of service provided must go beyond the expectations of the borrower. We must read between the lines of the request or inquiry, with an eye toward offering more than is seemingly being sought. The goal must always be to conclude the interaction with the feeling that the borrower left with more than he expected. These are human engineering "credits" we build up over time that can be used to our advantage later on if the need arises.

THE MOST EFFECTIVE COLLECTORS ARE THOSE THAT GENUINELY LIKE PEOPLE

The actual process of collecting amounts past due is a function of the interaction between people. It is certainly supported by ever advancing technology, but it always gets back to the people factor. The dialogue exchanged between borrower and creditor's representative has the potential of being very uncomfortable and, in fact, this seems to be the goal of many collection operations. The belief is that if the borrower can be made sufficiently uncomfortable, he will bend to the creditor's wishes and the matter will be resolved. This theory may appear valid intellectually, but it fails to take into account the factor of human nature. Purposefully creating discomfort for the borrower causes communication breakdown and resentment — anything but the desired result.

By way of illustration, it is not unlike a southern prison farm of long ago where prison guards would take pleasure in administering beatings capriciously to the prisoners. Over time, a prisoner came to realize that if he would just hunker down, the guard ultimately would tire of the activity and turn his attention elsewhere. Similarly, a borrower being verbally "abused" will hunker down by putting up a communications barrier until the collector tires of the exercise. Nothing positive comes from either effort.

Because of the potentially unpleasant nature of most collection contacts, it is important that they be handled in a graceful fashion. This is a skill that does not lend itself to being learned, but one that derives from a genuine like of people. Thinking that the skill can be simply learned usually will be met with a less-than-sincere assessment and woefully inadequate result.

THE MOST EFFECTIVE TOOL A COLLECTOR CAN POSSESS IS SALESMANSHIP

Salesmanship is the ability, skill, or technique of persuading another to one's own way of thinking. Thought of in these terms, a collector is every bit as much a salesperson as one who makes a living selling, say, life insurance. In fact, collecting an account has many parallels to the selling of life insurance products.

The challenge of a life insurance salesperson is that he is selling the prospect something intangible. The object of the sales effort is financial security for the insured's family that will not materialize until after his death. Of course the security translates into tangible dollars, but not from the perspective of the individual laying out monthly premiums. To him it is nothing more than an abstract idea — one that may be very difficult to accept. Just ask anyone who sells life insurance.

Similarly, the collector is not dealing in tangibles; he is selling an abstract idea. The idea, of course, is that to keep what he has the borrower must direct some of his resources to the curing of his mortgage delinquency. There isn't necessarily any particular gratification for the borrower, inasmuch as he is not receiving anything for the funds expended; he is being merely allowed to retain what he already has. And this is not the only selling challenge confronting the collector. He is attempting also to persuade the borrower while at the same time influence is being exerted on him by his other creditors. Remember, the borrower usually has resources to satisfy some of his creditors, and he must decide just who it is that will be paid — a decision that, as we have learned earlier, is based more on emotion than reason.

With so much emphasis placed on salesmanship, it should be clear that the most successful operations seek individuals who have had some success in sales or who have the type of skill set that will make them good salespersons. Moreover, it is important to expose the collection staff to sales training, including the skills necessary to overcome sales resistance. And, last but not least, if the collection staff is to be viewed as a sales force, it should be compensated like one. To the extent that an environment can be established whereby the collectors are allowed to think of themselves as salespersons, and where goals and compensation can be expressed in the same manner as would occur in a conventional sales organization, productivity will increase by virtue of the reinforcement of a positive self-image.

GETTING SOMEBODY TO *WANT* TO DO IT

Since the borrower is guided more by his emotions than his intellect, the challenge for a collector is to get the borrower to feel that he *wants* to cooperate — not that he *should* cooperate. The obvious concept is that a borrower should resolve his mortgage delinquency to avoid the disastrous consequences; but, as we have learned, applying the cognitive approach is usually ineffective. *Wanting* to do something always has a greater force of energy behind it than merely believing that something *should* be done. This concept becomes clearer as we take a closer look at the borrower's state of mind.

By having the ability to compartmentalize his problems, the borrower can coexist with them. If he weren't able to do this, he would be in constant psychological pain or discomfort — a condition he will avoid at any cost. We can illustrate this point by drawing an analogy to somebody in hospital who is suffering from chronically severe physical pain. The hospital patient is on a morphine drip to get him through the days and nights. Without it he would not be able to tolerate his condition.

As we have seen, the borrower has his own version of the morphine drip that he believes to be necessary for him to tolerate life. He wants to avoid his pain more than determining how his problem should be solved. He is "hooked" on pain avoidance every bit as much as the patient may be "hooked" on the morphine. So what the collector must attempt to develop with the borrower is a program of pain management.

We certainly would not consider the most effective means of pain management to rip out the patient's morphine drip and expect him to go "cold turkey." Similarly, giving the borrower a "dose of reality" by threatening him with the dire consequences of continuing to ignore his financial obligation is just as inappropriate.

The objective that must be achieved with the borrower is to get him to believe his situation is indeed manageable; that it does not have to be a case of extremes — the hopeless condition or complete avoidance.

Any daunting task, when viewed in its entirety, can seem like a hopeless undertaking that causes significant discomfort. Such tasks must be broken down into their component parts, at which point segmental solutions can be developed that collectively result in ultimate success.

Of course, no problem can be solved, segmentally or otherwise, until the borrower is willing to recognize that there *is* a problem. In this connection, he must be transitioned from his compartmentalizing denial back to reality. However, as already mentioned, this cannot be done properly through any sort of shock treatment. It must be pursued through more gradual means. Using the analogy, it is more like pinching off the morphine drip than unceremoniously removing it altogether. As this is being accomplished, the borrower, with the help of the collector/counselor, is given the ability to realize that solutions do exist and that a viable plan of action is indeed within the realm of reality.

CONCLUSION

In the final analysis, good and sound collection methodology emanates from an understanding of human nature and an honest compassion for the human condition. It is only through a genuine desire to help people that the collector can be truly effective in his efforts to manage the assets in a subprime portfolio.

Craig M. Allen, Ph.D., is the founder of Delphi Structured Finance Corp., based in the United States, and Delphi Compagnie Financière based in Geneva, Switzerland, providing asset-securitization services on both continents.

Allen has helped to establish a new market in callable mortgage bond products in Denmark and (together with his partner, a Danish bank) has built a securitization team that has issued approximately $3 billion of actively traded new securities. Delphi has also developed a trade-finance product and, together with a German bank, has created a finance company with a portfolio of commercial-performance securities exceeding $300 million.

Prior to establishing Delphi, Allen was a founding partner of Aegis Holdings Corp. and president of Aegis Financial Advisors, Inc. He was responsible at Aegis for developing unusual niche securities.

Earlier in his career, Allen was with U.S. investment bank Bear Stearns & Co., where he developed the credit-enhancement capacity that allowed the firm to create rated securities from whole-loan (non-U.S. agency) mortgage collateral, and played an integral role in the development of the French asset-backed market.

Prior to Bear Stearns, Allen was involved in multifamily real estate, owned a small mortgage company in Dallas, Texas, and ran a small consulting firm. He taught courses in multivariate and nonparametric statistics as well as other decision-science courses at the University of Texas at Dallas.

Allen holds a bachelor's degree in psychology from Brigham Young University. He received a master of science degree in animal behavior, a master of arts degree in mathematics, and his doctorate in decision-making under uncertainty from Arizona State University (a special program involving the psychology, mathematics, and engineering departments).

Special thanks are due to Spencer Kimball for assistance with the section on "Loan Grouping and Neighborhood Membership Techniques." Thanks are also due Dawn Howey and Linda Allen for help in producing this chapter.

Chapter 4

Credit Scoring and Risk-Adjusted Pricing: A Review of Techniques

Craig M. Allen, Ph.D.
Chairman, Delphi Structured Finance Corp.
Président/Directeur Général, Delphi Compagnie Financière

Predictive credit modeling, it seems, has been a bit like El Dorado, the fabled city of gold sought by the Spanish conquistadores: ephemeral, always just over the horizon, yet promising wealth untold. Fortunately, however, the elusive goal — quantitative assessment of creditworthiness — is coming ever nearer to realization.

Credit scoring is not an easy problem. The goal is somehow to measure a potential borrower and, from that initial assessment, make predictions about the borrower's expected behavior. The underlying hypotheses of any credit-scoring methodology are that similar borrowers tend to behave similarly and that historical performance assists in predicting future performance. The difficulty, however, as will be shown in this chapter, consists first in framing the problem and then determining which borrowers are, for these purposes, similar to one another.

This chapter will show the early development of credit assessment as a traditional credit-scoring problem, then expand upon that view to illustrate the techniques that are being utilized to explore more difficult credit problems, such as those associated with subprime lending. The traditional approach to credit scoring will be illustrated mainly from a conceptual viewpoint (that is, visually via exhibits). More modern techniques for credit assessment will also be examined from a conceptual viewpoint, spelling out the summarizing principles.

MEASUREMENT

This task of credit assessment is, at the outset, a problem of measurement. And, like all measurement challenges, the first two issues to consider, those that form a foundation for this craft, are reliability and validity.

Reliability

For measurements to be reliable, they must be repeatable. Not only must the data contributing to the measure be objective (in the sense that most observers would ascribe a similar value) but the measurement process (that is, the calculation steps) must produce a consistent result. A credit-scoring process that repeatedly measures identical (or essentially similar) borrowers, should produce identical (or essentially similar) results. Further, presuming that the attribute of creditworthiness is something relatively stable (allowing us to predict behavior two or three years into the future), such a measure for the same individual should not vacillate wildly from month to month. This sounds easier to achieve than is the case in actual practice, and bears some discussion at the outset.

An assessment of similarity among borrowers (that is, a good credit score) should be based upon directly observable variables, such as the number of months at the current residence, months at the current employment, number of dependents, debt payment history, monthly income (although here it starts to get subjective), current levels of debt, and other obligations. These directly measurable variables are the beginning of a reliable credit-scoring process. But, as one might guess, even many of those seemingly observable measures require a good deal of subjective input. Usually, in implementation, the actual borrowers' real-life situations give rise to more complex interpretations: Should irregular income be fully counted? What excuses exonerate previous delinquent payments?

These objectively based variables comprise only the starting point for a predictive credit measure. Only if consistency can prevail in the subjective determinations of the input variables could one hope for a reliable credit-scoring mechanism. Length, for example, is an inherently objective variable; but if the ruler by which it is measured is elastic and can be stretched by the observer, then the measured variable is not reliable even though the underlying concept of length suggests it should be so. This subjective capacity is a factor over which the scoring-model developers have no control. The adage, "garbage in, garbage out," is applicable, and poor management control of subjective decision-makers (or poor training) has frustrated many a scoring system.

The input variables are only a part of a reliable measurement system. The rest of the process, the calculation part, must also contribute to reliable measurement. Even when the ruler is inelastic, if our recording of length is done with inconsistent precision then differences between lengths will be unreliable. That would be the case if measurements were sometimes to the nearest centimeter, other times to the nearest thousandth of a centimeter and other times to the nearest inch). For another example, the area of a rectangle might seem to be an inherently reliable attribute: If both length and width are meticulously measured, and area is calculated as the product of these two, one would expect a reliable resulting measure. Suppose, however, that the calculator used to compare the areas of two rectangles operates to only one decimal place of precision; the resulting calculations may not reliably recognize differences in area.

In like manner, other factors can degrade the reliability of a credit measure. Too heavy a weighting of short-term variables may cause large changes in assessments of creditworthiness from period to period, when none, in fact, may be justified. For example, the salesman, paid largely by commission, may have income some months that is disproportionately large or small. Such short-term fluctuations should be weighted appropriately with longer-term trends in order to obtain a relatively stable credit assessment.

A reliable measure, then, is based upon objective criteria, or, when subjectivity is required, with consistent application of the subjective principles, with appropriate intermediate calculations, and upon an appropriate mix of both long- and short-term variables.

Validity

The other fundamental issue to consider when dealing with a measurement problem is one of validity: Does the measure really tell us what we think it is telling us? History books (and Monty Python movies) are full of examples of reliable measures that simply are not valid. Intelligence (whatever that is) was once believed to be predictable by measuring the size of the cranium. A witch was thought to be detectable by the presence of warts or by tests of floating on water (or, in parody, by comparing weight to that of a duck). Regardless of how reliable or repeatable these measurements are, a fundamental question to ask of credit-assessment techniques is one of their validity.

The fundamental hypothesis of predictive credit models is that similar borrowers tend to behave similarly. Ergo, valid methods had to be developed for aggregating applicants reliably into groups that were somehow "similar" with respect to credit performance. The first and most natural method of doing this is to group borrowers into categories of "good" and "bad." Surely the good borrowers repaid their loans and the bad borrowers did not. However, as is the case with detecting a witch, detecting a good borrower is a daunting task; often the testing process has lasting consequences. Just as non-witches were defined *post hoc* as those who float when tied up and thrown into a pond (with permanent consequences to the one tested), bad borrowers are often only defined *post hoc* as those who default on their debt (with permanent consequences to the lender).

Early credit scoring, in general, attempted to classify borrowers prospectively into groups of good and bad payers and not simply do so retrospectively; the classification needed to sort borrowers reliably into groups that were valid predictors of a future event's probability. Thus good and bad borrowers became predictive labels, suggesting something about propensity to repay debt.

'Good Borrower' Detection

Although the credit-scoring concept has moved much beyond the original notion of distinguishing good from bad credits retrospectively, it is useful to examine the original purposes that recognized the need for such a score. Along with the natural development of this model, certain assumptions will creep into our thinking. After reviewing the development of the traditional credit model, we will examine these assumptions and discuss why a conceptual shift has been necessary to expand our thinking of credit scoring to apply to the subprime markets.

It is easy to picture the desk-thumping bank president demanding that his loan officers make only good loans to good customers. Credit committees, to this day, tend to reach a conclusion that a customer to whom a loan is granted is a good credit. But the underlying idea that is being expressed is really one of relative probability.

Strangely, it was the early development of radio that gave us the roots of modern credit scoring. In those early days of poor reception dominated by static, it was important to develop a theoretic framework for detecting signals amid the noise. This theory of signal detection validates itself by measuring such things as hits, misses, false alarms, and correct rejections. Moving this to our credit context, we create a matrix as shown in Exhibit 1

We can use this matrix to monitor our decision-making effectiveness. Obviously, it is the hits (correct detection of a good borrower) and correct rejections (of a bad borrower) that we are attempting to maximize. And we want to minimize the misses (a good borrower that we mistakenly categorize as bad) and the false alarms (a bad borrower that we mistakenly categorize as good). As each application is examined, the underwriter attempts to determine whether this is a good borrower (the signal) or just another bad one (the noise).

Exhibit 1: 'Good Borrower' Detection Matrix

		Borrower Categorization at Time of Application	
		Good (grant loan)	Bad (reject loan)
Actual Borrower Category	Good (won't default)	Hit	Miss
	Bad (will default)	False Alarm	Correct Rejection

Different business objectives create biases in decision-making. If we are an originator, paid by volume of loans we approve, we may be biased to grant a disproportionate number of loans (increasing too greatly the false alarms or defaults). Similarly, if it is our money that is lost when a loan defaults, we would be biased to reject a disproportionate number of loans (increasing the misses or lost lending opportunities). The mathematical developments of the 1950s allowed objective measurement of these biases, but they will not be addressed in this work.

Also within this framework of signal-detection theory, a variety of broader statistical tools began to be developed for discriminating between signal and noise populations. These coincided with the improvement of radio receivers that were able to tune in more precisely on individual frequencies. These same tools proved to have useful application in credit decision-making and provided the fundamental tools for development of the traditional credit-scoring approach. This approach would lead to an initial validation framework for credit-scoring methods.

Practical Implementation

One of the early objectives for the credit score was practicality. The empirically derived credit score had to be made available at the point of credit decision-making. Since the early credit-scoring technology was first created in the 1950s, prior to the advent of affordable and readily available computers, the real breakthrough was in creating an easily computed score that could be practically implemented.

In that era of "prime" lending only, the task was one of recognizing those good borrowers who would have the lowest incidence of default. A simple scorecard method was introduced that assigned various point values to variables that were collected on the loan applications. These positive and negative point values resulted from simple operations such as multiplication of an objective borrower variable by one factor, another variable by another factor, or lookups of correct point values. The credit score was the result of summing the total number of points. The time required to calculate the score was just a moment or two, and the required mathematical ability was well within the level of any professional loan officer or underwriter.

This easy-to-use scoring method put a powerful, statistically derived tool in the hands of credit decision-makers. An objective and quantitative method was put into service to help the decision-makers justify their credit decisions. The method was reliable and, with the collection of hit and false alarm rates at different credit-score values, it took the first steps toward validation. Default rates for those borrowers with high credit scores were demonstrably lower than for those of borrowers with low scores.

Changing Environment Places Different Demands On Credit Scores

Since the days of those early credit scorecards, many aspects have changed. The market no longer seeks just those borrowers with the best credit. The requirement has evolved to predictability of cash flow, not just low default rate. Several credit businesses today, in fact, cater only to poorer credits — those that the original credit scorecards would have rejected.

The market for credit is built upon predictable flows of cash. While the payment flow of nondefaulting borrowers is routine, also predictable are the aggregate flows of large samples of borrowers who are less creditworthy (or so have several credit companies posited). Consequently, to the extent that a predictable set of flows exceeds the yield requirement established, credit companies have sprung up to capture those flows as loans. Certainly, the loans to lower-credit borrowers have characteristics (such as higher coupons) that compensate for payments missed because of defaults. But predictability of cash flow is the driver of modern credit decisions, not simply the predicted absence of defaults.

Another development that has changed the demands on a credit-scoring process is the relatively low cost and easy accessibility of computers. The virtual ubiquity of the personal computer has trivialized the calculation requirement that was important to the success of the scorecard approach. Very complex and difficult calculations can be easily and practically performed at the point of credit decision-making by lowering the requirement from "human calculator" to that of data entrant.

Chapter 4: Credit Scoring and Risk-Adjusted Pricing

These developments have, together, given birth to a new generation of scoring technology that provides not just a measure of borrower quality but an actual prediction of each loan's expected performance. Such technology, which directly estimates a potential borrower's performance, is often described as predictive modeling or risk-adjusted pricing rather than simply a credit-scoring system.

Through the development of this second generation of credit modeling tools we are able to separate ourselves more fully from the assumptions that initially constrained us. But let us begin with a review of the traditional approach. This will be followed by a critique of its assumptions and, finally, with the introduction of the second-generation tools.

A CONCEPTUAL REVIEW OF THE TRADITIONAL CREDIT-SCORING APPROACH AND METHODOLOGY

As discussed earlier, the underlying challenge in credit-scoring is to measure reliably some set of features of each member in a population of borrowers that results in a meaningful prediction of the borrowers' credit performance. The measurement process converts the assessment task into a mathematical problem that is easily and visually understandable. The concepts, but not the mathematics associated with this process, are developed in the following sections.

Quantitative Mapping

Reliable measurement begins with objective, quantitative mapping of the characteristics of borrowers. Specific rules precisely determine how each instance of a variable is transformed to a number. Age, for example, can be mapped as months since birth at the time of loan application. Income, as another example, may be subdivided into the variables of reported income and verified income, each with specific rules determining how various types of monetary inflows are to be counted.

Certain variables may be qualitative in nature, such as the answers to: Have there been previously reported bankruptcies? Such yes/no variables are quantified by substituting a value of 1 for one occurrence, 0 for the other. Other qualitative variables that feature a list of alternatives are best thought of as a sequence of yes/no variables with each yes/no alternative represented by either a 1 or 0 value in the list.

Upon completing the quantitative mapping, each potential customer is represented as a series of numbers; as a row of values, with each column representing a different measure of that customer. For statistical purposes, it is useful to think of these measurements in terms of rows of customers and columns of variables.

A typical list of variables might begin with the examples shown in Exhibit 2.

Exhibit 2: Typical Abbreviated List of Borrower Variables

> Age of borrower in months
> Number of dependents
> Months at current residence
> Months at current employment
> Length of time this line of employment
> Owns residence (y/n)
> Works full-time (y/n)
> Mailing address same as residence (y/n)
> Cash down-payment amount
> Gross monthly income
> Gross other income
> Verified gross monthly income
> Verified debt ratio

While the variables in this list are provided only as an example, some appear very commonly in actual credit models. Added to this list might be co-borrower variables, if any, or measures taken from a credit report, if such information is obtainable. It is important to point out that certain legal restrictions may apply to the type of information that may be used in developing a credit score (race and gender, for example, may not be used in making credit decisions in the United States). Also — in the U.S.A., at least — age may not generally be used in making credit decisions. But if such age measurement is part of a quantitatively derived credit model, there may be instances when it can be used provided that it does not contribute to discrimination against the elderly. Each jurisdiction may have its own laws associated with information use, and should be verified before implementing a credit model.

Once a suitable list of variables is selected (which list may contain, in some cases, as many as 200 or more different measures), the magic of mathematics takes over.

A Spatial Representation of the Problem

Each customer, as measured by the several variables, can be thought of as representing a specific point in the many-dimensional variable space depicted in Exhibit 3.

Exhibit 3: Plot of Borrower Characteristics In the Space of Two Arbitrarily Selected Variables

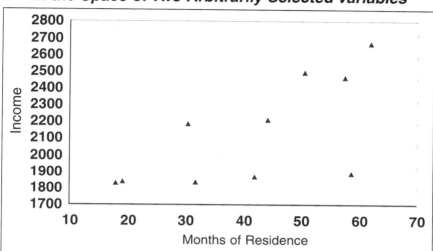

Exhibit 3 illustrates several customer data points when plotted in two variables. As the number of variables increases, the dimensionality of the space in which the customers are represented increases. When represented in this multidimensional variable space, customers who score similarly on the several variables tend to be near to each other.

For example, the two loans near to each other in the bottom left of the graph would be considered similar in these two dimensions. Similarity of two borrowers is merely a reference to the similarity of the values of their variables (or their proximity to each other in the variable space). And, since the assumption that underlies all credit scoring is that similar borrowers tend to behave similarly, the proximity of the two borrowers (in the lower corner of Exhibit 3) would lead to a prediction that they would have similar credit performance characteristics.

Driven by 'Good' versus 'Bad' Distinction

The development of a traditional credit-scoring model is easy to understand when approached from a graphical perspective. The basic approach, if you will recall, attempts to discriminate good (nondefaulting) loans from bad (defaulting) loans. Two samples are taken, one of borrowers that have defaulted and the other of borrowers that did not default but paid off their loan at maturity. Although, as discussed earlier, the defaulting and the nondefaulting borrowers usually are mixed together and overlap, a large sample of defaulted loans is likely to have a concentration of data points in one or more regions, and a sampling of the nondefaulting loans is likely to have a concentration of data points in other areas.

Traditional credit-scoring models usually presume that all nondefaulting borrowers constitute one population with a single mean, and, similarly, that all defaulting borrowers also constitute one population with a single mean. While these assumptions are not generally true in an absolute sense — particularly not when dealing with subprime populations — for the sake of this model development the assumption is made. It is often interesting to observe just how robust these assumptions turn out to be, however, when used to detect prime borrowers, as was their original use.

In general, the main principle underlying development of the traditional credit score is that nondefaulting borrowers and defaulting borrowers, although hopelessly mixed together, are thought to represent different populations of individuals. These populations are considered to have different characteristics or means, but the range of values associated with each variable or variance is thought to make it very difficult to discriminate one from the other — except in retrospect!

The Linear Discriminant Function

A sample of good and bad loans is identified to begin the development of a linear model for discriminating between the two supposed populations. The linear model becomes the scorecard that produces the specific credit score for an individual. A general appreciation for the process will be discussed in this section, without going into the more formal mathematical aspects of the statistics.

As described earlier, the two populations of borrowers (those that default and those that do not default) are considered to be different (that is, the means of the distributions are different). But because the variance found in each variable measure is generally large, the actual populations overlap considerably. The task is to distinguish between the two. In general, this would be considered a classification problem; that is, one is interested in making an observation of a borrower and then correctly classifying that observation as belonging to that which defaults or that which does not default.

In building the traditional scoring model, the variance is considered to be "normal" (That is, the typical bell-shaped curve studied in our statistics classes applies.) Exhibit 4 illustrates the concept of two different populations having different means, but with enough variance to

Exhibit 4: Two Borrower Populations

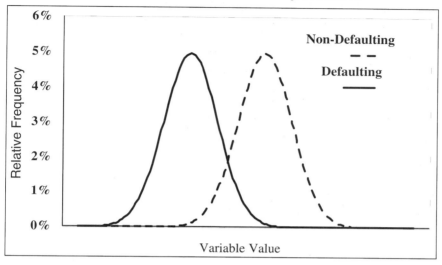

cause the two populations to blend. It is the overlap of the two populations — nondefaulting and defaulting — that makes the classification task difficult.

In Exhibit 4, which deals with just one variable (or one dimension, as we are wont to call it), a solution to the dilemma of distinguishing between the two populations can be readily seen. It would be possible to create a decision rule, or criterion point, that divides the two populations as meaningfully as possible. Although a debate could rage about exactly where to place that cutoff point, it would generally be between the peaks of the two distributions.

One typical solution would be to place the dividing criterion for the two populations at the point where the two distributions seem to dive into one another, as is the case in Exhibit 4. Borrowers scoring to the right of this point would be classified as nondefaulting and those scoring to the left of this point as defaulting. By placing the criterion at this intersection, as it is drawn, one maximizes the probability of correctly classifying an observation into its appropriate population. The intersection of the two probability functions implies that the two alternatives are equally probable.

However, in credit decisions, the cost of making a bad decision might create a bias away from simply wanting to be most frequently correct in the classification process. (With some thought, it is apparent that for borrowers falling right at this point of intersection, half of the loans are expected to default.) The cost of defaulting loans may bias one's opinion away from accepting a 50% default rate (at the point of intersection), and create a criterion point that has a somewhat smaller percentage of observations that are expected to default. The criterion for smaller default rates would be to the right of that point of intersection. This would, of course, mean that some good borrowers are rejected, but this bias would ensure that at the criterion point more than half of the borrowers will not default. Exhibit 5 illustrates this concept in two dimensions, and allows us to see one other issue that should be considered.

Exhibit 5: Two Multivariate Populations

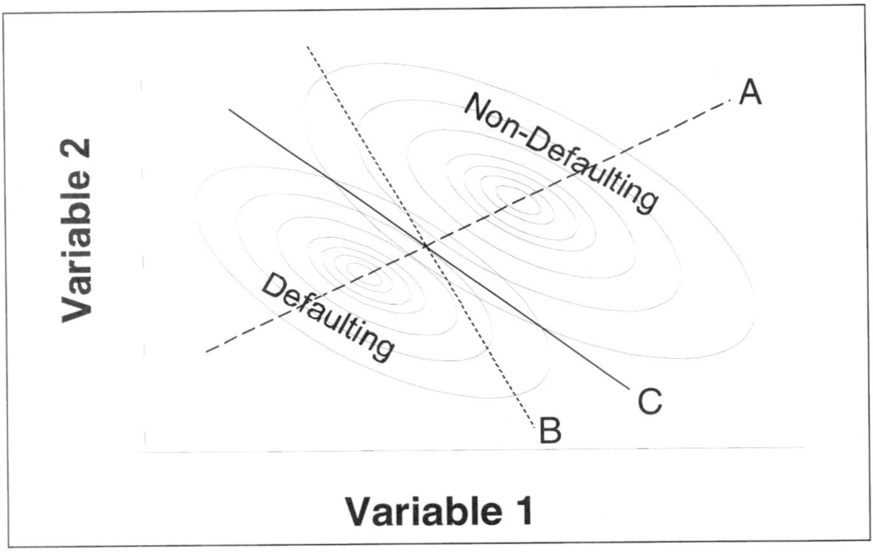

Exhibit 5 represents a population of nondefaulting borrowers and a population of defaulting borrowers as concentric ellipses, which indicate curved distributions much as a topographical map would indicate the shapes of two hillocks. The two populations overlap, or are mixed together as in Exhibit 4, represented by the intersecting curves describing their shapes.

In seeking to discriminate between these two populations, one must consider not only the locations of the means of the population but the variance and covariance as well. The two populations in this figure, defaulting and nondefaulting borrowers, have means that are connected by the dashed line **A**. One might view line **A** as simply a way to rotate the two-dimensional case into another one-dimensional case identical to that illustrated in Exhibit 4 and select a criterion point as described earlier.

However, because of the multidimensional nature of the two populations and their shape (that is, the covariance of the variables measured), selecting a criterion point is not enough. One must also select the angle, or tilt, of the criterion rule (in a two-dimensional problem the criterion is a line, in three dimensions, a plane, and so forth). The dotted line **B** is perpendicular to (or "orthogonal to" as a mathematician might say) the line **A** connecting the means. This line **B**, however, obviously would not be a good criterion line because it is evident that in the lower part of the figure it would include a disproportionate part of the defaulting population relative to the part of the population included in the upper part. The solid line **C** is rotated to take into account the covariance of the populations and maintain a balanced division between the two.

In general, for discrimination tasks of multiple dimension, a surface is selected that has the position and rotation required to divide the populations appropriately, as shown in Exhibit 6.

Exhibit 6: Two Multivariate Populations

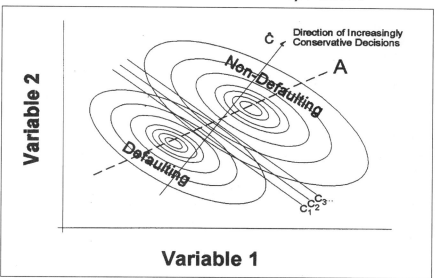

The positioning of this surface is adjusted so as to include only an acceptable probability of incorrectly classifying a defaulting borrower as nondefaulting. Exhibit 6 presents a series of such lines, C_1, C_2, etc., that would be increasingly conservative about the inclusion of defaulting borrowers among those deemed nondefaulting. Each of this series of criterion surfaces is parallel to the others and, for a credit-scoring system, the direction of increasingly conservative decisions is arbitrarily chosen to be positive (in the direction of the nondefaulting borrowers).

As may now be apparent, the direction $\hat{C}$, which is simply a line pointing generally in the direction of the good borrowers in the multidimensional borrower space, is really nothing other than a credit-scoring function. This process of determining the surfaces C_1, C_2, etc. and the function described by the line is called, in statistical terms, the development of a linear discriminant function between the two populations.

Calibration of Function for Expected Default Rates

Once the linear discriminant function is determined, a fully functional credit-scoring model is obtained by adjusting the zero point and the scale of the function so that, when calculating the value resulting for each borrower's variable values, a value consistent with credit-scoring conventions is obtained. Values, for example, are usually expected to be between 0 and 1,000, with certain score values corresponding to a certain level of expected defaults.

Some model developers would seek consistency with other models that they have developed and would attempt to calibrate the values of their various discriminant functions so that a score of 620, for example, would more or less predict approximately the same percentage of defaults across all of their models. This is often called the calibration process for the model; it attempts to make historical comparisons of credit scores roughly comparable from population to population or from year to year.

Difficulties and Limitations Associated with Traditional Credit-Scoring Systems

Although the traditional credit-scoring model has been shown to be quite effective in separating the extremely good credits from the extremely bad, there are a few difficulties and limitations associated with these systems. The first to be addressed deals with the conceptualization of the problem and the theoretic framework itself.

The most serious problem, as alluded to earlier, is the basic assumption that all defaulting borrowers come from a single population with a common mean and that all nondefaulting borrowers come from another single population with a common mean. This would imply that the borders between the defaulting and nondefaulting populations are smooth across many variables. As is particularly the case with subprime populations, these borders are *not* smooth — and significant interactions are very often found among variables — making some combinations much

Chapter 4: Credit Scoring and Risk-Adjusted Pricing

more susceptible to higher default rates than traditional credit-scoring models would predict.

Each of the significant problems associated with the traditional credit-scoring process is addressed in this section. Some of these problems are shown to be simply tradeoffs made for computational simplicity and really do not cause serious difficulties — especially when used with prime borrower populations. Other problems, however, are more significant and contribute to the need for the new generation of credit-modeling techniques.

Single Populations with Smooth Borders

Experience with subprime populations of borrowers reveals that the shapes of borrower populations that default and those that do not default are quite complex. This is illustrated in Exhibit 7.

Exhibit 7: Groups of Borrowers Plotted in 2 Dimensions

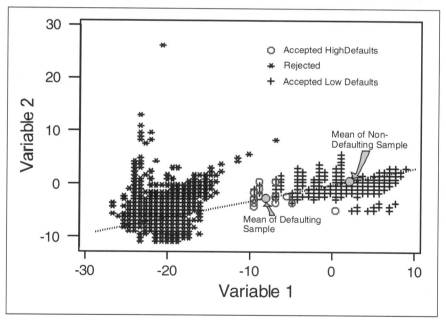

In Exhibit 7, each symbol represents a group of approximately 300 actual customers, plotted along two arbitrary variables associated with information on their loan applications. The asterisks, primarily in the lower left of the figure, represent groups of customers who were denied credit by underwriters evaluating their applications. The crosses and the circles represent groups of customers whose applications were approved and who were ultimately granted credit for an automobile loan.

The symbols for those groups accepted for credit are further divided into two groups, as follows: At the lower left of the main cluster is a relatively flat clustering of circles representing groups of borrowers who demonstrated high default rates. The remaining cross symbols represent borrowers with relatively low default rates. It is striking that both the groups of borrowers deemed worthy of credit and, then again, those experiencing the highest default rates, appear to be clustered together. It is a confirmation of the basic assumption of predictive credit modeling that such clusters emerge (similar borrowers behave similarly). The features measured by the two variables actually do reveal some similarities that translate into a predictive ability.

It should be pointed out, however, that within almost every group of borrowers — even those in the low-default-rate groups — there were borrowers who defaulted on loans. Similarly, within even the groups showing the highest default rates there were loans that did not default. In fact, defaulting borrowers are so thoroughly mixed in with nondefaulting borrowers that it would be impossible to ever state with credibility that such and such a loan will, with certainty, default; or will, with certainty, not default. These figures simply show trends and tendencies, that are measured only with different probabilities.

It is also apparent from Exhibit 7 that the shape of these populations is rather complex. The gap between the population rejected for lending and that granted loans is shaped by the underwriting criteria. However, the population of those granted loans with the higher and lower default rate is shaped by the vagaries of the variables themselves. It should be apparent that the borders between the higher- and the lower-default-rate groups are not smooth. (Although the criterion for dividing between high and low default rates was arbitrary here, at virtually any decision rule the same jagged borders are observed.)

Sampling Dependencies of Credit Scores

The protrusions and evaginations of the populations of higher- and lower-default-rate borrowers create another problem, one of sampling dependencies. As was illustrated in Exhibit 7, the contours for any given default rate within the borrower population are not smooth, as is the assumption with traditional credit scoring. Instead, there are bumps and valleys along the various variables. This has a tremendous effect on the traditional credit score development.

Exhibits 8a and 8b illustrate a population of potential borrowers, those to the lower left, marked with a circle, will have the higher default rates. Those to the right, marked with a cross, will have the lower default rates. If the underwriting criteria are such that the group indicated in Exhibit 8a is granted loans, then the population of defaulting borrowers would have a mean marked by point B_a, and the nondefaulting borrowers would have a mean marked by point G_a. This sampling of defaulting and nondefaulting borrowers would give rise to a discriminant function C_a with credit score function $\hat{C}_a$.

Exhibit 8a: Credit Score as Function of Data Sampled — Larger Sample from Less Conservative Underwriting

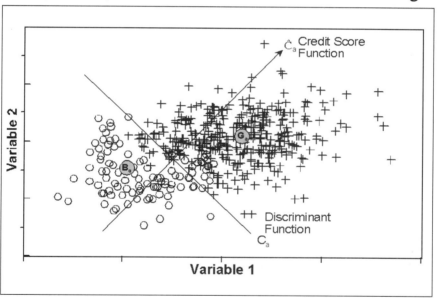

If, on the other hand, the underwriting criteria were such that the group indicated in Exhibit 8b were granted loans, then the population of defaulting borrowers would have a mean marked by point B_b, and the nondefaulting borrowers would have a mean marked by point G_b. This sampling of defaulting and nondefaulting borrowers would give rise to a discriminant function C_b with credit score function $\hat{C}_b$. The different credit scoring functions $\hat{C}_a$ and $\hat{C}_b$ are an artifact of the underwriting.

In fact, as underwriting changes and even as market penetration changes, credit score functions will change. The population from which borrowers are drawn exerts a tremendous influence on the "direction" of the credit scoring function. This is an unfortunate artifact of the traditional scoring framework. As will be shown below, however, the second generation techniques of risk-adjusted pricing have overcome these shortcomings.

Exhibit 8b: Credit Score as Function of Data Sampled — Smaller Sample from More Conservative Underwriting

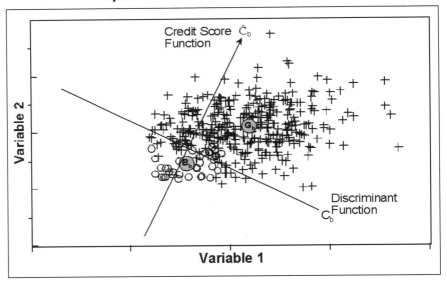

Single-Dimensional Score: Simplicity versus Loss of Information

It is useful to mull over one of the underlying premises of the traditional credit-scoring approach, that there is a single direction in the borrower variable space that captures the essence of being a good borrower. The lines $\hat{C}_a$ and $\hat{C}_b$ in Exhibits 8a and 8b and the accompanying discussion earlier in this chapter illustrate the rigidity of this concept. Provided that the assumptions about the single mean for the defaulting and nondefaulting populations, their normal distributions, etc., are roughly true, this single direction should generally point in the direction that maximizes discrimination between the defaulting and the nondefaulting populations.

However, even with these assumptions there is an obvious simplification made when all borrowers are aligned and projected onto a sin-

Chapter 4: Credit Scoring and Risk-Adjusted Pricing

gle dimension. Exhibit 9 shows two groups of borrowers, **V** and **W**, which lie at the same "credit score" value (both on the same perpendicular line C) but which might have very different group characteristics.

Exhibit 9: Two Multivariate Populations

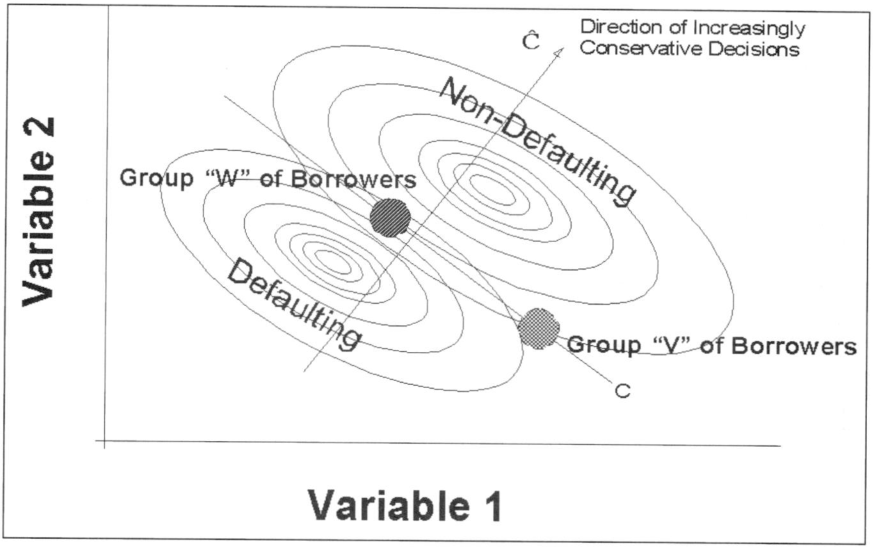

[Figure: Contour plot with axes "Variable 1" and "Variable 2" showing two overlapping elliptical populations labeled "Defaulting" and "Non-Defaulting". Group "W" of Borrowers and Group "V" of Borrowers are marked on a line C, with an arrow indicating "Direction of Increasingly Conservative Decisions" along axis Ĉ.]

The simple credit-scoring model compresses all of these groups onto the same one-dimensional measure (C) and ignores any differences among them.

The loss of information when all groups are projected onto a single dimension has been studied, and information theory provides a mechanism for measuring this loss.

Information has a formal definition that can be seen intuitively. If one thinks of the variability in the original borrower data (that is, the 50 or 100 variable measures on each borrower, which we can call the original borrower space), and how that variability is preserved as one attempts to map these data back and forth into another space. For example, one could map the borrower data from the original borrower space into the one-dimensional credit score space (using the credit score function), and then attempt to map back into the original borrower data space. One can compare the variability in the borrower data after performing this mapping, back and forth, to the original variability in the data prior to such mapping.

Mathematically, one can determine the maximum amount of information that could possibly be preserved by mapping from the original borrower space to any single dimension by measuring the ratio of the greatest eigenvalue of the borrower covariance matrix to the rank of that matrix. These are mathematical terms, perhaps forgotten or barely learned by most, that may best remain in the domain of statisticians. The reader need not worry that any portion of this chapter requires an understanding of these terms.

For one specific (and rather typical) population of 93,000 borrowers, with 39 variable measures, this process showed that at most 12.32% of the information about the borrowers could be preserved by mapping onto a one-dimensional space.

This suggests that a credit score, while simple to calculate and generally useful in discriminating between a defaulting and nondefaulting population, does so with great loss of information. The simplification of the problem into the typical credit scorecard will toss out the majority of the information about the borrowers (approximately 88% in the example cited). The resulting, simplified measure of the borrower fails to discriminate between or among many borrowers who may, in fact, be very different from each other.

Subprime Lending Is Interior-Focused

Another difficulty associated with the typical credit-scoring model arises in its application to the nonprime borrower. The traditional credit-scoring technology was developed in the days when discriminating between the best borrowers and the worst borrowers was the required task. The marketplace has changed, however, so that today's subprime lenders do not seek the best (prime) credits but, rather, *acceptable* credits. The typical use of a credit score among subprime lenders is to make subtle discrimination among borrowers who are all nonprime, attempting to find neither those that are extremely good nor extremely bad but, simply, to find those who are somewhere in between — who will not default as frequently as others.

The traditional credit-scoring models are based on the premise that one is intending to maximize the likelihood of distinguishing between good and bad credits. And, as indicated, too often this is not the use to which they are put. Consequently, when one attempts to use these standard credit models in subprime lending, it is a bit like using a socket wrench to drive a nail or a hammer to remove a bolt. While the models may work in a crude sort of way, they are simply the wrong tool. As shown below, however, the proper tools do exist and they are very effective at solving the problems for which they are designed.

Monotonicity: A Dangerous Generalization

One final assumption implicit in the traditional credit scores is that the credit function is essentially monotonic (or smoothly progressing from the worst to the best credits). While it might be easy to observe that all borrowers with a score of 700 are better credits than those with a score of 400, the models also predict that all borrowers with a score of 550 are better credits than those with a score of 545. Experience, unfortunately, tells us this is simply not the case.

Instead, experience tends to indicate that credit scores in the mid-range are not very predictive. In other words, in the precise range sought by nonprime lenders, credit scores do not foretell accurately which loans will perform better than others. The credit scores are helpful in identifying the borrowers as nonprime but, beyond that, it is difficult to make further discrimination.

The credit score's focus on *extrema*, as explained earlier, is one reason that this occurs. A good example might be seen in a variable such as number of dependents. The typical credit score would most likely give some positive weighting to this variable (such as adding three points for each dependent child). However, experience has shown that some circumstances (perhaps a single parent, marginally employed borrower) may suggest just the opposite. The credit score's immutability attempts to use what is generally true in predicting the performance of *every* case.

The inability of credit scores to take into account special circumstances, especially those that seem intuitive with actual lending experience, has made many users wary of incorporating this sort of predictive model. As nonprime lenders come to realize, each type of borrower is really a different special case, and the monotonic tools that work for identifying the best borrowers are actually limited in their predictive abilities — in just the range that is most needed.

TECHNOLOGY ADVANCES: PREDICTION BASED ON SIMILARITY AND ACTUAL HISTORY

Technology to overcome the limitations of credit scoring, as described earlier, has become available as the cost of computational power has fallen. It is now feasible to approach predictive credit assessment from an entirely new, but inherently simpler, perspective. This new approach, known as data mining, has actually been made possible by advances in data-processing techniques. The presumption of data mining is that the best method for predicting performance of a loan is simply to use the history of previously made, similar loans.

The actual methods used may vary but, essentially, when a predictive assessment of the creditworthiness of a loan is sought, an enquiry is made to the loan history data base. A group of similar loans is identified, complete with their history since origination. The summarized information of these peers is used to predict the behavior of the new loan.

The prediction of each new loan's behavior, with these techniques, is based not upon a theoretical relationship developed from a sample of good and bad loans (as is traditional credit scoring) but upon actual experience. The advantages of this approach are numerous.

Measurement Using the Neighborhood Approach

The major conceptual hurdle to overcome when modernizing one's view of credit assessment is really nothing more than a change of perspective. Instead of grouping all defaulted loans together and seeking the average location of defaults (as is done with traditional credit scoring), one groups borrowers into something akin to a neighborhood and determines frequency of default (and other measures of loan performance). Thus, the task becomes a two-step process of aggregating into groups, then measuring the attributes of those groups.

Although the aggregation of borrowers into groups, as a matter of practical implementation, precedes the measurement of the attributes of the various groups, the discussion of grouping techniques will be deferred. Instead, we focus on conceptual issues first and leave the discussion of the techniques actually used to the final section of this chapter.

Imagine the original, two-population view used in developing the traditional credit score model, as pictured in Exhibit 10.

Instead of dividing the population into two groups — those that defaulted and those that did not — and then trying to determine the location of greatest concentration of each group (the credit-score method), imagine that we arbitrarily divide the population into several small groups (without respect to their loan performance). Exhibit 10 shows this division with the grid overlaying the borrower distributions. (In reality, the subdivisons are much, much smaller.)

Now, we actually measure what has occurred historically within each group (or neighborhood). We make no assumption about there being only two populations (good and bad credits) nor do we presume that there is a smooth transition from good to bad. We do not even have to limit our questions to default rate. We simply find the group of borrowers about which we are interested and then measure the attributes of concern.

When a new borrower is presented, this methodology simply identifies the neighborhood to which the borrower belongs and then reports the expected behavior of that borrower's group. It is simply the opposite perspective of the traditional approach (group, then measure versus the old, divide by defaults, then find division function). This approach sets us free from some of the troubling assumptions and limitations of the older methods.

As will be shown, this methodology is enormously useful with subprime populations. In practice, it also proves very interesting with prime borrower populations (which are well served by traditional credit scores) because multiple attributes can be measured.

Exhibit 10: Two Multivariate Populations Gridlike Division into Smaller Populations

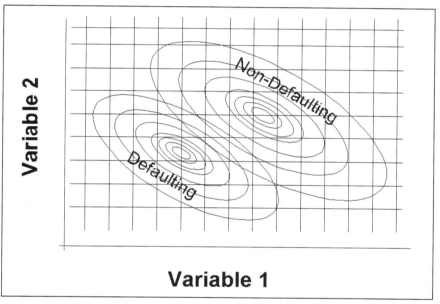

Default Survivorship

As we recall from the development of the traditional models, a credit score defines a measure of discrimination between two presumed simple populations; those that default on loans and those that do not. Unfortunately, that is not what subprime lending is all about. Subprime lenders seek to predict the cash flows that will result from a loan and make an economic decision about whether or not to fund it, depending upon the timing and magnitude of the loss expected. While a credit score may be related to these aspects, it is simply an altogether different animal.

Using the neighborhood approach, each group that has been defined is measured. There may be nine groups or there may be nine hundred groups of borrowers defined. Each of these is examined and the profile of actual defaults within the group is assessed. Usually, this measurement is performed with respect to timing of default and percentage of loans that have survived default through each period.

Since the loans that fall into each of these neighborhoods have usually been originated at different times, a rough function is calculated that identifies the percentage of loans of age t or older that have survived. Exhibit 11 illustrates such a function.

Exhibit 11: *Actual and Estimated Monthly Default Rates*

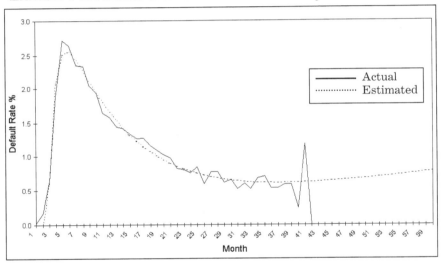

In calculating this function, one normally observes that there are many loans of age one month or older, a bit fewer of age two months, fewer still of age three months, and so forth. This is because a portfolio (from which one measures) is dynamic. Often, after a certain age, the number of loans observed that are of that age or older becomes very small. When the number of loans for such time period is small, the estimate of the percentage that survive to that age becomes unstable. Consequently, several compensation techniques have been developed.

What is important to note, however, is that each neighborhood is characterized by its own individual default survivorship function. Thus, when a new borrower is presented, the neighborhood to which it belongs is examined. The precise function of defaults is determined by the history of other, similar borrowers and this default function is applied to the new borrower as the best predictor of that borrower's performance.

Other Measures

Just as expected default frequency is adjusted for each borrower based on the history of his or her own neighborhood, other measures are also adjusted. Often, there are delays associated with repossessing collateral or variations in collateral condition that manifest significant changes within borrower neighborhoods.

Using the neighborhood method, virtually any measure of interest can be determined for a group of borrowers. The changes in values sometimes appear to vary systematically from one part of the population to another and, sometimes, the measures appear to have local clusters of values with higher values centered in particular areas. This becomes quite useful when making predictive models. For each neighborhood the future behavior of each loan is predicted by the history of each of the loan's peers within that cluster.

This ability to assess each measure of interest separately and to do so independently of any predetermined assumption — as is the case with traditional credit scoring — gives this second generation of predictive models extraordinary versatility. This category of tools is usually called data mining, because the history for each group is mined out of the existing historical records of similar loans.

Avoiding the Pitfalls of Monotonicity

Among the greatest advantages of this data-mining approach is elimination of the assumption of monotonicity. Instead of presuming that there is a smooth transition from the best credits to the worst, this approach recognizes that relationships among the borrower variables may vary. At some income levels, the debt-to-income ratio may be more predictive than at others or the number of delinquencies on previous debt may be more predictive.

This approach eliminates the relationships that are hard-wired into a credit score, such as: $300 of additional income increases the credit score by the same amount as six months of additional time of employment. There is no presumption of any consistent relationships among the borrower variables. Instead, the simple historical performance of similar loans provides the framework for estimating the future performance of a new loan.

Assessment of credit by identifying a group of similar loans and using their performance as a guide is a very pragmatic approach to predicting behavior. The primary assumption is reduced to that basic generalization of credit prediction: Similar borrowers tend to behave similarly. The problem is simplified into one of assessing only the similarities among borrowers.

Conceptually, this is very much like the approach used in appraising the value of real estate. Within a particular neighborhood, comparable properties are examined to determine such factors as sale prices and income-producing capabilities. In this approach to credit assessment, however, comparable borrowers are sought whose history is understood and they are examined to provide insight about credit-related behavior. And, just as in real estate appraisal, the selection of those to whom the comparison is made is critical to appropriate valuation.

The New Problem: Assessing Borrower Similarity

Recalling the fundamental premise of all credit modeling, that similar borrowers behave similarly, it can be seen that increasingly sophisticated tools are being used to identify similar groups of borrowers which then are used to predict credit performance. Perhaps the most promising advances in this area deal with multidimensional representations of borrowers.

Similarity, as has been used intuitively up until now, has really meant proximity in the variable space of the borrowers. A distance measure between two points is directly substitutable for the concept of measuring how alike two borrowers might be. When both borrowers have a credit score of 574, they are considered alike. However, that single measure of credit score has limitations, as developed earlier; the predictive models used in subprime modeling expand on this concept of similarity.

It should be pointed out that a precondition to comparing variables which have widely different values and ranges (as in income, which is measured in thousands of dollars, and income ratios, which are measured in fractions) the variables are usually normalized. This most often means that from each variable the average of that variable is subtracted and the difference is divided by its standard deviation. This makes all normalized variables with a mean value of 0.0 and a standard deviation of 1.0, which are more readily comparable with each other. Each normalized borrower variable is then an indication of how many standard-deviation units that value is above or below the average value for all borrowers.

The second-generation credit approaches usually begin with the acknowledgment of the shortcomings of a traditional credit score and the subsequent development of another measure of something else that seeks to incorporate additional borrower variables. An example might be seen in those companies that have built and used a general credit-scoring model that utilizes certain variables on a loan application. But, realizing the additional information about the borrower that is provided by an extensive credit report, which is not fully utilized in the original credit score, they build another credit report score that incorporates much of this otherwise unused information. These companies then use both the original credit score and the credit report score to predict borrower behavior more effectively.

Because of the additional information that is utilized in predicting borrower performance, these two-dimensional or three-dimensional models often significantly enhance lenders' forecasting ability. However, the *ad hoc* addition of supplemental credit scores does not always assure a better predictive model.

The general approach of multidimensional representations of borrowers and multiple measures of credit performance has been shown to be a very productive and an exciting direction in credit modeling. The best approaches rely upon a more rigorous approach and certainly point the way for future credit-score development.

Correlated Variables and Information Retention

The specific problems that credit scores, in general, seek to overcome, and that multidimensional models of borrowers solve, deal primarily with two related issues. The first is that, in trying to represent borrowers in some meaningful way using credit variables obtained at loan origination, the serious statistical problem of nonindependence arises: Certain borrower variables tend to be highly correlated. The second problem is that, in eliminating some of the redundancy in the correlated measures, information can often be lost.

If a distance or similarity measure between two points is taken as its simple Euclidian distance (the square root of the sum of the squared differences of each variable), then adding a new variable to the distance measure will change the estimate of similarity. If that new variable is simply a restatement of an existing variable, the distance measure will increase even though no new information is added by that variable. Although this argument has a mathematical basis, the redundancy problem can be examined from a more intuitive basis.

The problem of nonindependence among variables is primarily thought of as a messy statistical nuisance, but it complicates even a conceptual understanding of the data. Variables that are not independent change together; as one variable changes, the likely range that another variable takes on tends to change as well. Models that utilize only one of these variables might identify effects associated with that variable but, if two nonindependent variables are used for prediction, the effect tends to get blurred between the two variables. This is analogous to the relationship between number of points scored in an intramural basketball league and height of a player. One might notice the same relationship between points and the vertical reach of the player when jumping. Since height of player and jumping reach tend to be related, one might reasonably have difficulty determining whether the scoring relationship is due to height or jumping reach or some combination of the two.

Some companies, for example, develop measures of borrower income. One of these measures might be monthly income as reported by the borrower; another might be the verified income from the underwriter, who calculates income only by using specific rules. A credit modeler might argue that reported income and verified income both measure the same thing and only one of them ought to be included in the credit model. This would, however, be wasting the information provided by the differences between the two variables. Indeed, both income variables do tend to measure the same thing (and hence are highly correlated), but credit evaluators also value the slightly different information provided by both measures and often include both in a credit model.

The solution for the problems associated with highly correlated or nonindependent measures are easily resolved mathematically, but can also be seen with the following simple, intuitive example. One can argue that two variables are required to utilize fully the information in two correlated but slightly different variables.

The credit modeler could create two new variables; the first might be the average of the verified income and the reported income and the second might be the simple difference between them. The first of these variables represents the major attribute purported to be measured (that is, how much this person makes). The second of these variables represents the disparity between the two measures (a reality check of the borrower's perception of his income).

In this example, it is important to note that the two highly correlated income variables are easily represented with a single, composite variable reflecting the primary attribute of both, but only with the loss of information. In order to retain all of the information, another variable needed to be added — that part of the information not conveyed in the single, composite representation.

In general, many of the borrower variables tend to be highly correlated. For a statistician, the composite variables used to represent these correlated measures are called principal components.

Concept of a Principal Component Space

In the earlier example there were two different measures of borrower income: that reported by the borrower on the loan application and that determined by the underwriter after investigation. Exhibit 12 represents a typical set of data for these variables and illustrates the composite or principal-component variables discussed earlier. It is with these principal components that the basis of similarity measures among borrowers are established.

Exhibit 12: Reported versus Underwritten Income

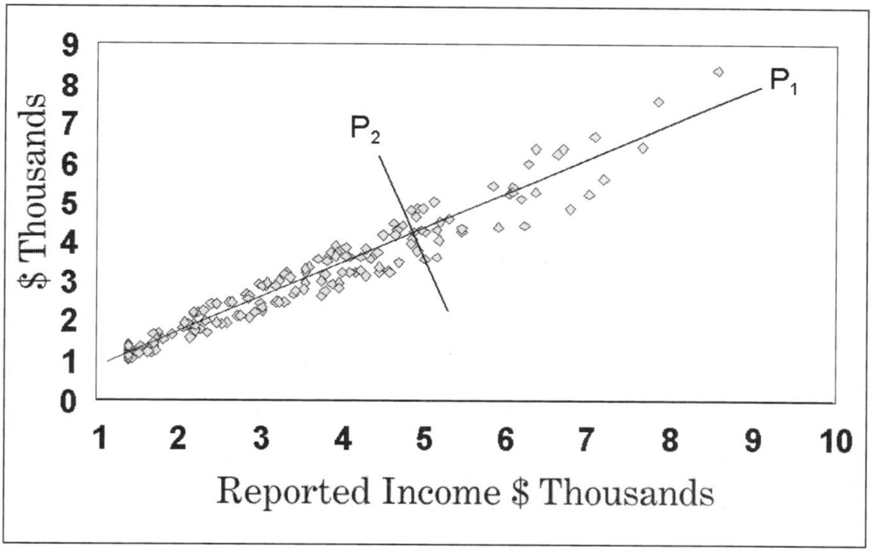

[Scatter plot showing Reported Income ($ Thousands) on x-axis (1-10) versus $ Thousands on y-axis (0-9), with principal component line P_1 along the major axis of the data and P_2 perpendicular to it.]

The first of the principal components in Exhibit 12 is the line P_1, which follows along the major axis of the sample of these two income measures. This line, P_1, can be seen to capture the general information in both variables. The data plot shows that as reported income increases, the underwritten income tends to increase, and this general relationship is captured by the line P_1. Since it captures the primary relationship between the income measures it is usually considered the "first" principal component of the variables.

This first principal component is related to the correlation between the two variables. The slope of this line P_1 is very similar to that which would be predicted by other statistical methods such as regression analysis, which would attempt to extract the relationship between these two variables. Principal component analysis is a much more general tool, though, than regression, in that it can be used to extract the relationships among several variables at once, without some of the assumptions of regression. When the data sample includes more than just two measures, the principal components are determined by the correlations among all of the variables. The first principal component might then be thought of as pointing the direction of the major correlation among all variables.

As the major relationship of these two income variables is represented by the first principal component, a name is usually given that reflects as much. The first principal component in this example of Exhibit 12 might thus be referred to as the income factor or something similar.

As can also be seen in Exhibit 12, there is another line, P_2, that is perpendicular to line P_1. This corresponds to the second principal component. This (and any subsequent components extracted from higher-dimensional problems) represents that portion of the overall data variance not explained by the first principal component.

Conceptual Issues in Factor Weightings

Usually, in principal component analysis, the borrower variables are represented in a table with a factor associated with each of the principal components. An actual factor-weighting matrix which has been sorted by coefficients might be as represented in Exhibit 13. The data in this exhibit are sorted so that the variables are in descending absolute magnitude with respect their coefficient labeled PC_1. Only the first six, largest principal components (PC_1 - PC_6) are presented in this exhibit, although 13, in actuality, exist.

Each borrower variable (in its normalized form) is multiplied by the coefficients in the matrix and the column sum provides the value of each principal component. The column PC_1 in this exhibit supplies the coefficients for the first principal component, PC_2 for the second, and so on. In this way, the 13 variables associated with each borrower allow the borrower to be mapped into the principal component space. This principal component space has the desirable property of each dimension being orthogonal, or perpendicular, to every other dimension. Thus, distance measures for similarity have meaning.

In Exhibit 13, the row "eigenvalue" indicates the relative importance of that principal component in describing the overall variance of the portfolio. In this example, the value associated with PC_1 is approximately 3.3, and it accounts for about 25% of the total variance in the data. The second principal component accounts for approximately 12%, and so on.

The coefficient for each variable in each principal component is related to a factor weighting. For these purposes, a factor weighting can

Exhibit 13: Sorted Matrix of Principal Component Coefficients

Name	ID	PC1	PC2	PC3	PC4	PC5	PC6
Verified Gross Monthly Income	12	0.52174000	0.48751800	0.00627757	-0.03483180	0.08380410	0.13072800
Owns Residence	6	0.16060600	0.03802040	0.32072500	0.18612900	-0.24855400	0.24466200
Age of Borrower	1	0.12445100	0.16953500	0.48895700	-0.03895760	0.14511000	0.12878600
Months at Current Residence	3	0.05925460	0.07275670	0.58234600	-0.03651820	-0.16853800	-0.01605290
Number of Dependents	2	0.05520240	-0.00042608	-0.03719940	0.46557500	-0.00847272	0.16164700
Gross Other Income	11	-0.03975870	0.07957660	0.02504140	0.02620630	-0.10148700	0.12900700
Cash Down-Payment Amount	9	0.03835860	0.36421200	-0.09298220	0.06017860	-0.06899970	0.04886870
Months at Current Employment	4	0.02890860	0.15408600	0.53678000	0.03271890	0.58222700	-0.09446200
Length of Time This Line of Empl	5	0.02736050	0.17886100	0.49299400	-0.00355669	0.42912300	0.03946330
Gross Monthly Income	10	-0.02062370	0.31272600	0.03990360	0.03179590	0.10827000	0.10466900
Mailing Address Same as Res	8	0.00819672	0.00906224	-0.07380480	-0.07637980	0.13626000	0.70543500
Verified Debt Ratio	13	-0.00762389	-0.01772890	-0.00920652	-0.00131319	0.00533494	-0.00168223
Works Full-Time	7	-0.00139017	-0.00367356	0.16182200	0.07437100	0.41152000	-0.23312800
eigenvalue		3.27592546	1.59581089	1.12245029	0.87204431	0.84775754	0.76458779
		25.1994%	12.2755%	8.6342%	6.7080%	6.5212%	5.8814%

These data comprise a subset of variables from a sample analysis and the eigenvalues have been modified for example purposes.

thought of as the weight, or importance, of each of the borrower variables in a principal component or factor. These weights are then used to help interpret or attach a meaning to each of the principal components. As indicated earlier, the variables in the Exhibit 13 are sorted by the absolute magnitude of their weightings in PC_1.

It can be seen that PC_1 has a very high weighting on the variable of verified gross monthly income; all of the other variables have significantly lower weightings. This would lead an analyst to identify PC_1 as simply a restatement of that one variable. PC_2, however, has relatively high weightings on a combination of variables: verified gross monthly income (once again), cash down-payment and gross monthly income as reported by the borrower. Thus, an analyst seeking to interpret or put a name to PC_2 might call this something like borrower liquidity. PC_3 has high weightings in variables associated with age, length of residence, and employment stability, so an analyst would more likely than not give this component an interpretation such as "borrower stability."

For each principal component, an analyst usually finds a name to help interpret the factor or general borrower characteristic that the mathematics are describing. The casual observer of this exhibit can, with only modest effort, attach somewhat meaningful names to the components and gain an intuitive feel for what that component measures. The true benefit, however, of the principal components is that each of these components is independent of every other principal component, and distance measures between points plotted in this principal component space are well behaved mathematically.

An Expansive View of Borrower Similarity

One of the benefits of having a rich mathematical basis for determining borrower similarity is that extensions to the categorization model are easily made and understood. One particularly valuable extension to the similarity model arises when looking at seasoned portfolios. Those familiar with Bayesian statistics might feel more comfortable than those with only a traditional statistical training when jumping so easily between and changing the definition of *a priori* and *a posteriori* events. If the reader feels uncomfortable about this jump, please bear with the following arguments and consider the approach on its merits.

In a seasoned portfolio, say one that has all loans of age six months or older, the performance of a loan during this common ageing period may provide loan grouping information that is useful in predicting future credit performance. One common practice is to examine a loan's first-month payment record. Those loans that become 30 days delinquent on the first payment are often intuitively grouped by portfolio purchasers and excluded from purchase. The mathematics of the approach described here allows several measures of borrower behavior during the ageing period (that the loans have in common) to be used quite simply in these models. The behavioral measures are applied, just as underwriting variables are used, in appraising the similarity of loans. Then, with these additional similarity measures, the historical performance of each loan neighborhood (from that point forward in time) is assessed. Different default rates and delinquency rates are often observed in neighborhoods defined, in part, by these early behavior measures.

It is the flexibility of this data-mining approach that allows each defining characteristic of a loan to be used, as might be appropriate, in obtaining a better and better estimate of expected borrower performance. Questions may be posited for subpopulations of loans — such as: What can be expected of loans aged 40 months or more? — which rely on the history of loans that have already aged beyond 40 months. Then again, the same question can be asked of loans aged 30 months or more. In each case, the behavioral predictors that occur prior to that 40th or 30th month can be used as additional variables in assessing the similarity of loans.

One example of a feature that has been used to aid in grouping loans is associated with delinquency type. Loans, for example, with a payment lapse of 60 days or more within the first N months of their life are tagged and event frequencies counted (N, of course, being chosen as appropriate for the population being examined, as described in the preceding paragraph).

Each occurrence is identified as either a lapse with recovery (delinquency followed by a catching up in payments so that the Nth month's payment due is received by month N) or a lapse with no recovery (delinquency followed by no catching up, and only the $N-2^{nd}$ month's payment due, or fewer, has been received by month N).

The number and category of each type of delinquency aids in grouping seasoned loans and enhances predictive ability for the remainder of their life. (For example, 24-month-old loans with two or more 60-day lapse-with-no-recovery delinquencies typically have a higher expected default rate than those with no 60-day delinquencies during their first 24 months, and so forth.)

The benefit of this approach is the unlocking of the richness of information contained in historical payment files. When properly set up and repeatedly updated (with each month's history added), this approach leads to a dynamic and self-correcting estimation system for loan performance. The calculations are intense, but the value of increased predictive ability usually outweighs the cost of the computer and analysis.

Loan Grouping and Neighborhood Membership Techniques

The aggregation techniques alluded to in the preceding sections are intuitively simple, but actually are quite challenging in implementation. The grid methodology that was used in describing the neighborhoods of Figure 10 suggests that the objective of these techniques is to establish some boundary within which loans are considered sufficiently similar to be grouped. Then, as indicated in the previous sections, these grouped loans are measured for performance attributes (such as default rates) and their group measure is used in some predictive model.

"Sufficiently Similar" The concept of "sufficiently similar" is the challenge. On an intuitive basis, we might seek to choose either some set of loans within a specified boundary in the borrower space or a set of, say, K of the most similar loans to a point, and use that set of loans as the definition of the neighborhood.

A Gridlike View It might be appropriate to begin with a gridlike view of the problem. It would be possible to look at each loan and determine the maximum and minimum value observed along each dimension. (Since we are using a principal component space, these will be referred to as PC_1, PC_2, and so forth up to PC_d — for d as the number of dimensions.) The range of values between PC_{1max} and PC_{1min} might be divided into some number of "bins," say 10, and loans falling into each bin of PC_1 could be grouped. If PC_2 is also included, then the 10 bins of that dimension together with the 10 bins of PC1 would make a 10-by-10 grid and loans falling into each of the 100 bins would be grouped.

So far, this approach might be seen as tractable. Certainly, some of the grid squares might be sparsely populated, others might be densely populated. If that were the only problem, something might be worked out to normalize the grid boundaries to distribute the borrowers more evenly within the grid. However, consider adding PC_3 and its 10 bins to make 1,000 boxes of 3 dimension, and then PC_4 with its 10 bins to make 10,000 hyperboxes of 4 dimension.

It can quickly be seen that neighborhoods defined with a grid-type approach will soon become unwieldy. The number of neighborhoods using this method for d dimensions will be 10 raised to the dth power. Even if 10 bins were not used, but only 2 values for each variable, this system becomes unusable because the number of grid-neighborhoods grows exponentially with the number of dimensions.

Defined Neighborhood Instead, the preferred approach is to chose the K nearest neighbors to a point as its defined neighborhood. This is illustrated in Exhibit 14 where each point is clustered with its nearest neighbors into a neighborhood, M_1, M_2, etc. If an originator wishes to make a prediction of a new borrower's performance, the K nearest neighbors to that new borrower would be identified as its defined neighborhood.

The value of K might be chosen for statistical significance. If K were set at 300, for example, the neighborhood of a new loan, and the basis for predicting how that new loan will behave, is the 300 nearest loans in the database to that new loan. Typical values of K are usually between 100 and 500. If too few loans are chosen to comprise the neighborhood, some estimates may be difficult to make with precision. The larger K, the smaller the number of neighborhoods and the less specific the predictions for the particular borrower. This is a fundamental trade-off that must be considered when using this approach.

For example, if the typical historical database of loans originated over several years is used, the following problem arises. A neighborhood of, say, 100 nearest loans is selected, and all 100 loans have a payment history variable (or conversely, a measure of whether they defaulted) in their first month of life. However, a few of the loans in the database would be only one month old, so the number of loans with a second-month payment history variable will be smaller than 100.

Exhibit 14: Clustering by Nearest Neighborhoods

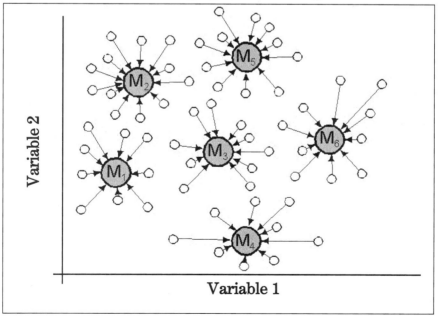

Similarly, because many are yet too young, fewer of the loans will have a payment-history variable for month 4, fewer still for month 20, and fewer still for month 40, and so forth. The number of loans selected for a neighborhood must be adequate to provide enough observations at the point of interest (expected defaults in months 48 to 54 of loan life, for example).

Direct Distance Technique In general, the distance technique has been shown to be superior to other methods of determining neighborhoods. Consequently, in data-mining applications such as this, one often speaks of nearest neighbors as the grouping technique.

Even this is a computationally difficult approach, but one which is tractable with appropriate algorithmic precautions.

SUMMARY

This chapter has examined predictive modeling of credit. It began with a reminder that both the reliability and the validity of an approach need constant examination. From that groundwork it has redeveloped the historical framework for quantitative models known as credit scores.

While simple credit scoring has been shown to be a useful tool, particularly in prime credit markets, it has been found wanting in some applications that require differentiation among borrowers that are not at the extremes (good or bad) of the credit dimension. The historical credit-scoring approach tends to lose validity when applied to marginal credit populations. When differentiating among various groups of borrowers which may not be the best of credits but are not so extremely bad that no credit is extended, other methods have been found more aptly applied, derived from the general field of data mining.

These data-mining methods are shown to rely on the fundamental assumption that similar borrowers tend to behave similarly. There are few assumptions about the orderly transition of bad borrowers into good borrowers. Instead a neighborhood approach is described that attempts to cluster similar borrowers into small groups. The historical performance of these small groups of similar borrowers provide the foundation for predicting the behavior characteristics of new borrowers.

With this method, the actual history of the K nearest neighbors to a new borrower is assessed. The default frequency curve, for example is determined by comparing the defaults of these K nearest neighbors to the aggregate default frequency of the population as a whole. If it is greater that the population average, then that new borrower is expected to default with similar greater probability.

Chapter 4: Credit Scoring and Risk-Adjusted Pricing

This approach, as developed in this chapter, results in a direct prediction of behavior, rather than the assignment of an intermediate credit score. Such direct prediction allows multiple measures to be used, in addition to the standard default prediction of credit scores. One further advantage of these new data-mining methods is that the technique lends itself to non-monotonic changes in credit quality. It permits a focus on the interior ranges of credit quality, rather than focusing only on the *extrema*.

As presented in this chapter, new techniques have been developed specifically for making credit predictions about the subprime borrower. These methods provide for increased predictive ability, precisely within the population where the previous credit models have been most disappointing. As these methods are more broadly applied and more widely understood within the subprime market, we can expect greater and greater confidence in this market's credit forecasts. To the extent that this confidence is shown to be merited, we can expect a reduction in the harsh judgments levied by the market in valuing subprime business.

John A. Costa joined Cardholder Management Services, L.P. in 1993 as managing director, planning and new business development, and was promoted to senior vice president in 1996.

CMS is a leading credit card servicing organization and the acknowledged expert in servicing subprime credit cards. CMS services subprime and secured credit card programs for several of the largest credit card issuers. CMS has also been an active participant in evaluating and purchasing distressed credit card portfolios.

Initially, Costa had responsibility for client development, co-branded marketing, and consulting on industry-related projects, as well as financial modeling. Today, he leads the sales and marketing effort for CMS and is responsible for establishing joint ventures and analyzing company investments in related businesses.

Prior to CMS, Costa was a financial consultant to various corporate clients in areas including mergers and acquisitions, financial modeling, asset securitization, and the establishment of creative lending facilities for off-balance-sheet funding. Costa has more than 10 years experience in asset securitization, including structuring and privately placing pass-through certificates and developing asset-backed commercial paper funding conduits. He is currently serving as a director of Litchfield Financial Corporation, a publicly traded specialty finance company.

Costa holds a bachelor of arts degree in English, Phi Beta Kappa, *magna cum laude*, from New York University.

Chapter 5

Credit Card Servicing for the Subprime Market

John A. Costa
Senior Vice President
Cardholder Management Services, L.P.

In the credit card industry today, a vibrant and disparate marketplace has evolved for consumers with either poor credit or no credit history. While the subprime credit card market has existed for over a decade, its growth has increased dramatically in the economic expansion following the Gulf War. This period of sustained economic growth has meant a gradual increase in the quality of life for most Americans, even those in the "cash" economy.

This backdrop is important for our discussion of subprime credit card servicing because, at its core, this is the story of how people outside of the traditional economy move into the mainstream of economic life. Subprime credit cards and other forms of subprime lending are symptoms of economic optimism by an emerging or recovering class. "A rising tide lifts all boats" — including, apparently, life rafts.

Unlike other forms of consumer lending, credit cards are both a loan device and an "access" device. That is, a credit card has utility beyond its lending function. (If you doubt this, try to rent a car sometime without a major bankcard.) In other types of subprime lending, whether auto or mortgage, the core concept is that the lender is making a loan to a less-than-creditworthy customer (or at least to one not generally considered creditworthy) and requires more collateral and more revenue to compensate the lender for the risk. In the subprime credit card industry, this statement is true, except that the lender generally does not extend any significant amount of credit. Whereas a subprime auto or mortgage loan is still primarily a loan, a subprime credit card is primarily an access device — and only secondarily a loan.

CATEGORIES OF SUBPRIME CARDS

Within the subprime category, there are two general types of cards. First is the traditional secured credit card which requires a cash deposit to collateralize the credit line. The second, and more recent type of card, is the high-risk "unsecured" card. While this type of card is technically unsecured, it generally has a very minimal credit line and, in some cases, most if not virtually all of the credit line is used to pay fees to the card issuer. This type of card will be described in more detail later in this chapter.

Given that the subprime credit card market is very different from the prime credit card market, what are the ramifications in terms of servicing the business? How different is the profit and loss (P&L) of a subprime card issuer as compared with the P&L of a prime issuer? What expertise must the servicer provide in order to maximize the opportunity for a profitable program?

FUNDAMENTALS OF CREDIT CARD SERVICING

A subprime credit card is still a credit card — and virtually all of the functions that a prime issuer must marshal are also needed to run a successful subprime program. But whereas prime issuers have built sophisticated machines that run "clockwise," the subprime servicing machine runs counterclockwise. This will become apparent as we review the key servicing areas of the credit card business.

Application Processing and Account Underwriting

The most successful traditional unsecured credit card issuers are masters of the application-processing and account-underwriting discipline. These issuers are typically highly automated, and can process applications with high speed and accuracy. Since most of these issuers exist within the traditional preapproved, direct mail paradigm, speed is important in several respects. In particular, the time between the initial prescreen bureau work and the back-end bureau review needs to be as short as possible. This is a reflection of the core underwriting task which is to assess credit risk accurately. While fraud is also a problem that major issuers must constantly address, most issuers have sophisticated systems in place to detect application fraud.

Fraudulent Activity Subprime issuers look at the application-processing and account-underwriting task very differently. First, the subprime issuer must be concerned about fraud. Fraudulent activity is in some ways a larger problem than credit risk in this marketplace. While that may seem counterintuitive, the rationale is that many thieves suspect that subprime issuers (and particularly secured card issuers) have a lower underwriting threshold and that they may be less diligent about ferreting out fraudulent applications. In many cases this is true, especially if the subprime card is handled in the same fashion as a prime card (for example, a prime issuer that handles a secured card program). Some unsophisticated secured card issuers assume that if the security deposit check clears, then they needn't worry about fraud. This is clearly not the case. A $300 security deposit does little good when a criminal ring takes the card overseas and manages to spend $30,000 before the account can be successfully closed. Most sophisticated subprime card issuers use extensive fraud-detection technology and may also use fraud investigators who manually review applications for certain handwriting clues and other patterns of fraudulent activity. Many issuers also maintain a database for known fraudulent addresses and other suspect application information, essentially creating a "negative file" as an additional level of fraud review.

Credit Underwriting While fraud underwriting is most significant, credit underwriting must also be carried out in an efficient manner. Credit underwriting is more fundamental in some ways. The expectation of the subprime issuer is that the applicant may not have bureau information or may have a record of past problems. (Most subprime issuers will not look favorably upon someone who is currently delinquent.) Subprime issuers need to be assured that the applicant is a real person, has a real address and phone number, is over 18, and has some minimum income. Some very sophisticated issuers, notably Capital One Financial Corporation and Providian Financial Corporation, have brought to bear their risk-modeling technology on the subprime market, but for the most part, risk scoring does not enjoy the same wide acceptance in the subprime market as it does in the prime market.

Cost If fraud is more of a problem, and credit scoring technology is not generally utilized, the third big difference between subprime and prime credit card underwriting becomes apparent: cost. Not only is it generally at least as expensive to underwrite a subprime account as to underwrite a prime account, but that expense represents a much greater proportion of the overall P&L. If a prime issuer has an account with an average balance of $1,600, expects an overall yield from that account of 20%, and paid $11 to underwrite and set up the account, the application-processing expense was over 3% of revenue. A subprime issuer might spend nearly the same amount and have expected revenue of only one-third as much as the prime issuer.

Customer Service
The largest card issuers have used customer service as a means of competing for and retaining valued clients. It is not uncommon for a large

unsecured issuer to have exceptionally high service-level standards and a high degree of uniformity in maintaining those standards. A recent research study of top-tier credit card issuers compiled by the Auriemma Consulting Group found that the mean ASA (average speed of answer) for these card issuers was less than 25 seconds for over 75% of their inbound phone calls, with some issuers actually answering over 85% within 20 seconds.[1] Equally impressive, the top service providers in this study had an abandon rate (i.e., customers hanging up before their call could be handled by a service representative) of 2.97%.[2] Clearly, the traditional credit card business has determined that customers need to be able to have their questions answered promptly, and most issuers provide this service level on a 24 hour-a-day, year-round basis.

What does this level of service cost to provide? For a large and efficient issuer, the cost of an incremental call can be approximated as shown in Exhibit 1

Exhibit 1: Cost of Incremental Calls

Cost per hour for customer service representative (CSR)	$10.00
Adjustment for nonproductive time	25%
Adjusted cost per hour for CSR	$13.33
Adjusted cost per minute	$00.22
Telecommunication cost per minute	$00.06
Inclusive cost per minute	$00.28
Average handle time (seconds)	198
Average cost per call	$00.92

The hidden cost, which is much harder to quantify, is what level of staffing inefficiency an issuer must support in order to maintain a desired service level. While sophisticated call-center models exist which predict what staffing levels are needed, based on historic call patterns, there is still a need to "overstaff" in order to maintain world-class service standards.

In the prime credit card business, a cardholder may call one or two times in a year. Based on this example, the unallocated call center expense for the prime credit card issuer may be $1 to $2 per year. The economics for the subprime issuer are generally much worse. The cost per minute is not appreciably different than the cost shown above, but

---

[1]This information is taken from a private study conducted by the Auriemma Consulting Group, Inc. 1400 Old Country Road, Westbury NY 11590.
[2]Ibid.

the average call is nearly twice as long. Moreover, subprime customers call much more frequently, easily on the order of 8 to 10 times per year.[3]

If subprime customers call 10 times more often and cost twice as much to handle, it is apparent that cost is as much of a problem here as it is in the application-processing/account-underwriting function. Fortunately, subprime customers do not demand the same level of customer service. That is, it is unnecessary to provide subprime customers with a 20-second average speed of answer. While extremely long hold times are expensive and frustrating, there is no need to overstaff to maintain the "world class" customer-service standard. While a platinum cardholder may leave an issuer if the service is substandard, a subprime cardholder is not likely to leave just because of a "long" hold time. The reality is that platinum customers receive new offers constantly, but subprime cardholders are largely beyond the reach of conventional direct marketing.

COLLECTIONS

When most observers think of subprime in terms of servicing, collections is the first thought for active participants in this market. This is, after all, a population that has a decided proclivity to treat bill payment as optional. In addition to the continual refrain (manage costs!), subprime collections again requires us to rethink our objectives.

In the traditional unsecured card business, collections is actually more crucial since there are more dollars at risk. Many sophisticated issuers have developed elaborate strategies to make sure that delinquent accounts are categorized and treated according to the level of risk that they represent. Such issuers have employed high-powered technology (such as collections scoring models or predictive dialers) and have embraced outsourcing, even if only as a "challenger" to their in-house collections area. These issuers use multiple measures of collection productivity, but chief among them is the calculation of "roll rates."[4] The gener-

---

[3]We are referring to calls handled by a customer service representative on a mature portfolio. Calls to a voice response unit (i.e., to check available credit, etc.) can be much more frequent. Calls on a newly originated portfolio are also much higher until the cardholder establishes certain behavior patterns with the issuer.

[4]A "roll rate" is the percentage of accounts or dollars that were delinquent this month expressed as a percentage of the accounts or dollars that were delinquent the prior month, measured by stage of delinquency. For example, if there are 500 accounts that are two cycles delinquent and last month there were 1,000 accounts that were one cycle delinquent, the roll rate would be 50%. That is, the likelihood of an account that is one cycle delinquent this month becoming two cycles delinquent next month is 50%.

al goals of the collections area for the prime issuer include: collection of past due amounts, restoration of accounts to good standing, preventing further deterioration in roll rates, arresting the increase in additional borrowing (i.e., managing the open credit line), and minimizing the amounts charged off. A detailed discussion of collections strategy is beyond the scope of this chapter.

If the average subprime issuer has a small dollar exposure to a delinquent account, what is the driving motivation behind the collection effort? What part do late fees and penalties play in the collections strategy? How much effort is appropriate?

Even though subprime issuers may have only a small actual exposure to the cardholder, they also have a large vested interest in terms of cost to acquire and originate the account. In addition to the cost to process the application and set up the account, there was a cost to acquire the account. (Assuming that direct mail was employed and assuming an average cost per item mailed of $1, a 0.5% response rate[5] means that there was a $200 acquisition cost.) Not only are these costs high compared with an unsecured card, they are high as a percentage of the revenue available from the subprime card account. Viewed in this way, the collection effort is in good measure a retention effort. Late fees and penalty rates are also a key component of the overall collection strategy for the subprime accounts. These fees can be a very significant part of the overall revenue available to the issuer. (A $29 late fee is nearly 10% in yield on a $300 balance!) The critical issue in understanding the fee versus effort tradeoff is that a large portion of these fees will be uncollectible. Understanding this at the outset is important since the way these fees are treated during chargeoff can lead to misleading results (particularly in the case of secured credit cards).[6] Taking these two perspectives into consideration, the collection effort should be focused on keeping those accounts that are viable rather than chasing all accounts for what may be, in reality, a small principal "exposure."

---

[5]This is a hypothetical example only. Many issuers that have attempted to originate secured cards, in particular, through direct mail have had notoriously bad response rates well below the industry averages for unsecured card mailings.

[6]For example, assume a secured card issuer has a $29 late fee and a $15 overlimit fee and charges off after 180 days past due. A secured card with a $300 balance and a $300 security deposit, after six months of delinquency, could have a balance of $549 (six late fees plus five overlimit fees). If, during the chargeoff process, the security deposit is applied as a "payment," it could easily be applied first to the $249 in unpaid fees, resulting in a "chargeoff" of $250! This treatment would overstate income and overstate chargeoffs as opposed to reversing the fees out of income and reducing the amount of the chargeoff to 0.

PROCESSING AND SYSTEMS INTERFACE

The credit card industry has done an exceptionally good job at driving processing costs to the lowest level possible. While card processing is sometimes viewed as a commodity, the actual utilization of the processing system is one of the "bright lines" separating cutting-edge issuers from behind-the-times issuers. In fact, one of the most important responsibilities of the servicer (whether the cards are serviced with the bank's own staff or the bank utilizes an outside service provider) is the design and implementation of the processing system. Most of the major processing systems available have extensive features that allow a high degree of customization for specific card products and programs.

In the prime card business, systems design and parameter settings can focus on maximizing revenue, minimizing risk, retaining and rewarding profitable customers. In general, the subprime issuer has many of these same goals, but needs to utilize different parameters particularly as they relate to risk.

Most unsecured card issuers provide credit upon payment posting, in which case insufficient funds (NSF) checks become an exception item and are often redeposited. In the subprime world, and particularly in the case of secured cards, there is often a need to restrict the credit available from a payment for several days in order to make sure the payment check has cleared. Subprime issuers that have not utilized this type of "payment float" strategy are easily defrauded by check kiting against the account.

For example, a secured cardholder with a $300 credit line sends in a payment of $5,000. Unless a payment float, or similar tool, is utilized upon posting of the payment there is a large credit balance that the cardholder can access and spend. After the $5,000 payment "bounces," this generally becomes a frantic, and often unsuccessful, "skip trace" effort. Other areas where systems tools can be especially helpful to a subprime issuer include authorization settings, collections entrance parameters, and "neural net"-driven authorization pattern fraud detection.

MISCELLANEOUS SERVICES

There are numerous other services and subsystems that are involved in the credit card business. In addition to the remittance processing example discussed earlier, the subprime card issuer needs to carefully develop its management information reporting system. For example, a subprime issuer needs to be especially sensitive to the available credit in the portfolio. Whereas prime issuers institute fairly regular line-increase programs and credit line review programs, the subprime issuer needs to do this on a case-by-case basis. Some subprime issuers offer a "graduation" to an unsecured credit line after maintaining an account in good standing for a certain period of time. In general, this "time based" graduation is less than optimal. Other subprime issuers offer to continually review the account for credit increases based upon demonstrable improvement in the cardholder's credit quality.

In addition to the line management process, subprime issuers also need to carefully monitor the cardholders' spending patterns and payment patterns. Beyond the controls used to manage the payments of the subprime cardholders, it is also advisable to control the amount and timing of cash access to the credit line. Because subprime accounts generally have small credit lines, cardholders frequently make multiple payments in a month in order to keep a certain amount of available credit. This greater velocity can distort the principal payment ratios that most analysts calculate.

SUBPRIME MARKET OVERVIEW

Contrast to Prime Market

We have already discussed several ways in which the subprime market differs from the prime market. Exhibit 2 summarizes some of the main differences between the two markets.

Exhibit 2: Prime and Subprime Markets Compared

	Prime Credit Cards	Subprime Credit Cards
Marketing method	Direct Mail	Telemarketing
Funding	Asset-backed securities	Self funding & deposits
Service level required	High	Moderate
Service intensity	Low	High
Collections intensity	High	Moderate
Average ROA	2%	5%
Average balance	$1,600	$400

Economic Profile of Consumer

If we use the Fair Isaac Company model as the credit scoring standard, we can approximate the credit range for the subprime versus prime cardholder. At the risk of vastly oversimplifying, most issuers consider a minimum FICO score of 670 as the entrance point for unsecured solicitations. The subprime region is best thought of as a FICO score between 550 and 670. In terms of income, most subprime issuers will have a minimum threshold of $10,000 to $12,000, and many will require at least one open trade line.

Prior Experience with Credit

In the subprime credit card business there is an adage:

> There are two types of subprime customers: those who don't understand how credit cards work, and those who understand too well.

Roughly half of the subprime population consists of emerging or new entrants to the credit markets. This includes not only young adults, but also immigrants and divorced women who may not have a credit file under their name. In general, this "thin file" type of account represents not only a good marketing prospect but potentially a future unsecured customer.

The "recovering credit," on the other hand, has had credit problems that may be attributable to illness, loss of employment, or simply financial irresponsibility. These cardholders will require substantial interaction since the issuer must help instill good payment habits where none existed. These accounts benefit from early intervention on the part of collectors.

SIZE OF THE SUBPRIME MARKET

There are various estimates of the size of the subprime market, but MasterCard has estimated that this may be a population as large as 25 million individuals. This is not a static population: New individuals enter this "pool" and others leave it every year. The ever-increasing tide of personal bankruptcy has been one steady contributor. These individuals are generally considered subprime for several years after their bankruptcy has been discharged.

Immigration to the United States is another major source of entrants into the subprime pool; some of these populations move readily into the prime markets while others take several years to become economically acclimated. For example, in recent years there have been many Russian immigrants to the United States who had been trained in their homeland as physicians, computer programmers, and other "professional" job categories; they take entry-level jobs as they are assimilating but often eventually move into a position that is closer to their experience level.

Types of Subprime Cards in the Market

As described earlier, there are two categories of subprime cards in the marketplace today. The first is the traditional secured credit card. While there are numerous variations on this structure, the basic secured credit card has a cash-collateral account held by the card issuer that, in most cases, is equal to the credit line extended. Some issuers offer larger lines (i.e., 150% of deposit) for larger deposits, but most hew closely to the 100% collateralization level.

The largest challenge associated with these cards is origination. While it may be easy to target the likely candidates for a secured credit card using conventional bureau-scoring and list-management techniques, this population is a notoriously bad responder to direct-mail pieces. Even those that do respond often send in an application with no deposit check. There are several reasons why secured card applicants frequently do not send in checks with their applications. One reason is a healthy skepticism. There have been several less-than-ethical issuers operating on the fringe of the law and many applicants are not sure they will actually receive a card after they send in a check. Beyond skepticism, it is simply difficult for many potential applicants to gather the cash necessary for the deposit. (Issuers that allow a low initial deposit have a much higher "take" rate.) For those that are willing to send in a deposit and have scraped together the necessary cash, there are some that do not have a checking account and, therefore, must buy a money order or use a money wire service.

The traditional secured card is often actually a good consumer value, particularly cards issued by major banks. These secured cards frequently pay a reasonable interest rate on the deposit, have a moderate annual percentage rate (APR) and annual fee. Unlike secured cards originated by telemarketing companies, most of the major bank-sponsored secured cards do not have an application or setup fee. Many of these issuers engage in the secured card market to satisfy branch demand and do not necessarily look at the product as a "profit center." These banks often have very tangible graduation plans in place.

The second class of subprime credit cards is the "high fee unsecured" credit cards. These cards, which are marketed mainly through telemarketing and television advertisements, turn the deposit notion on its head. These offers trumpet "no security deposit required!" but, in actuality, the applicant has only a negligible amount of unsecured credit available upon issuance. For example, a card may have a $250 credit line but have the following initial charges placed on the card: a $99 "setup" or joining fee, an annual membership fee of $75 leaving an "open to buy" of

$76. (Some offers of this type have fees so large that there may be as little as $1 of available credit.) While it may be easy to scoff at offers of this type, by and large they have met with a very high acceptance rate.

Why would a consumer choose a "high fee unsecured" card when a traditional secured card would seem an obviously better value? The main reason is that the high-fee unsecured card has a lower "all in" cash requirement. Whereas the traditional secured card requires the applicant to send in $250 to $500 as a security deposit, the high-fee unsecured cards typically charge all the fees to the card. This is done for two reasons: first, it lowers the cash requirement to the applicant and, second, it reduces the issuer's exposure by limiting the available credit to a very small amount.

IMPORTANT CONSIDERATIONS FROM THE CONSUMER'S PERSPECTIVE

The following items are the important considerations for most subprime applicants:

- How much cash is required? As discussed earlier, nothing is more pressing to the applicant than minimizing the cash expenditure.
- Can the cardholder graduate to a traditional credit card? How long will it take?
- Will anyone know that this isn't a "regular" credit card? Can it be used like any other credit card?
- Will using this credit card help establish or reestablish credit?

Typically, the consumer is not concerned about the APR or the fees charged by the issuer.

IMPORTANT CONSIDERATIONS FROM THE CARD ISSUER'S PERSPECTIVE

The driving consideration from the issuer's perspective is managing costs. Since the typical subprime card has a low average balance, and since the issuer cannot readily grow the balance because of the inherently greater credit risk in this subprime population, managing costs becomes extremely important. By and large, managing costs in this population means influencing and shaping customer behavior.

Some subprime issuers do not offer toll-free numbers. While the cost of providing the 800 number is actually quite small, the real cost savings is the reduction in call frequency. These issuers seem to be suggesting that the cardholder should not call unless there is an important reason. The more prevalent position, however, is that each customer phone call from a subprime population is an important opportunity to teach the cardholders something, remind them of something they may have forgotten and for the issuer to learn something new about the cardholders. Naturally, the issuers who take this position are not overly concerned about providing the 800 number service.

While managing servicing and processing costs is clearly important, the most important cost for the issuer to manage is the bad-debt cost. The chargeoff risk is the single largest expense component for most subprime issuers. For many of the high-risk unsecured card programs, it is not unusual to see gross chargeoffs in excess of 25% of the portfolio principal outstanding. Even in the secured card programs, assuming that the issuer has done a reasonably good job of limiting the overlimit and fraud risks, the incident rate of chargeoffs remains very high. In these programs, a high chargeoff rate can be viewed as a multiplier on the account acquisition cost. That is, even if the charged-off account does not present a principal loss to the issuer, it does represent an opportunity cost — since the issuer paid a price to acquire the account.

IMPORTANT CONSIDERATIONS FROM THE CARD SERVICER'S PERSPECTIVE

The most important consideration for the servicer in a subprime portfolio is managing the inherent instability in these populations and programs. The servicing tasks are all quantifiable, well understood actions that most servicers are capable of handling. Unfortunately, the low limit of available credit for these accounts exacerbates any normal servicing issues. A change in payment processing, for example, that might be completely transparent to a platinum cardholder could turn into a major problem for a subprime cardholder.

Even in the normal course of events, servicing subprime cardholders presents unique challenges, particularly in terms of call staffing. The servicer may find that their usual account-to-staff ratios are completely skewed and that a larger portion of their inbound calls do not terminate with the automated response unit help offerings. Astute servicers may also find that they need to maintain proprietary database information in order to optimize portfolio management. For example, the servicer may need to record and keep additional phone numbers used by cardholders (beyond what may be shown on an application).

In addition to a magnified call volume, subprime portfolios also generally result in a greatly increased collection workload. The usual collection entrance parameters may not be terribly useful here nor are the usual collection sequence of events. In general, most subprime issuers feel that early intervention is absolutely critical and that early referral to a recovery unit (whether internal or to an "early out" collection agency) is warranted.

SUBPRIME CARD PROFITABILITY

By now, many of the differences between the prime credit card arena and the subprime card business are apparent. Still, a side-by-side comparison of the respective P&L statements for the businesses helps clarify the important financial dynamics.

Comparing the P&L of a Subprime Card Issuer And a Prime Market Issuer

Exhibits 3 and 4 show the profit and loss statements of two hypothetical (but not atypical) portfolios, one for secured credit cards and the other for classic unsecured credit cards.

Exhibit 3: P&L for Portfolio A, Subprime Card Issuer

Assumptions			Profit and Loss Statement		
Average accounts	60,000		**Revenue**		
New accounts added in year	5,000		Interest	3,253,501	18.70%
Accounts 30-59 days past due	5,250	9%	Annual fee	1,500,000	8.62%
60-89 days past due	3,138	5%	Interchange	365,366	2.10%
90+ days past due	3,100	5%	Late fee	2,757,120	15.85%
Average active accounts	43,496	72%	**Total revenue**	**7,875,987**	**45.27%**
Number of phone calls	450,000		Cost of funds	521,952	3.00%
Average call handle time (seconds)	180		Processing expense	695,936	4.00%
balance per account	$400.00		Servicing expense		
spending per account	$600		Active accounts	561,098	3.23%
Acquisition cost, per new account	$50		Per-call charge	378,000	2.17%
Average loans Outstanding	$17,398,400		Early-stage		
Annual percentage Rate	22%		collections	603,936	3.47%
Revolving rate	85%		Late-stage		
Interchange rate	1.4%		collections	465,000	2.67%
Annual fee	$25		Application		
Late fee	$20		Processing	35,000	0.20%
Cost of funds	3%		Settlement	35,000	0.20%
Processing fees per account per year	$16		**Total servicing**		
Servicing costs			**expense**	**2,078,034**	**11.94%**
active accounts, per year	$12.90		Acquisition cost	250,000	1.44%
per-call charge, per minute	$0.28		Provision for		
early stage collections, per year	$72		loan loss	2,609,760	15.00%
late stage collections, per year	$150		**Total expense**	**6,155,682**	**35.38%**
application processing	$7		Pre-tax profit	1,720,305	9.89%
settlement & accounting, per year	$35,000		Taxes @ 40%	688,122	
Servicing cost per account	$47.78		**Net Income**	**1,032,183**	**5.93%**
Provision for loan loss	15%		**Expense summary**		
			Processing, per account		$16.00
			Servicing, per account		$47.78

Exhibit 4: P&L for Portfolio B, Classic Unsecured Card

Assumptions				Profit and Loss Statement		
Average accounts	60,000			**Revenue**		
New accounts added in year	5,000			Interest	8,019,900	11.73%
Accounts 30-59 days past due	3,200	5%		Annual fee	—	0.00%
60-89 days past due	2,400	4%		Interchange	1,596,000	2.33%
90+ days past due	3,000	5%		Late fee	1,548,000	2.26%
Average active accounts	38,000	63%		**Total revenue**	**11,163,900**	**16.32%**
Number of phone calls	76,000			Cost of funds	3,420,000	5.00%
Average call handle time (seconds)	120			Processing	608,000	0.89%
Average balance per account	$1,800			**Servicing expense**		
Average spending per account	$3,000			Active accounts	387,600	0.57%
Acquisition cost, per new account	$100			Per-call charge	42,560	0.06%
Average loans outstanding	$68,400,000			Early-stage collections	403,200	0.59%
Annual percentage rate	17.50%			Late-stage collections	450,000	0.66%
Revolving rate	67.00%			Application processing	35,000	0.05%
Interchange rate	1.40%			Settlement	35,000	0.05%
Annual fee	$—			**Total servicing expense**	**1,353,360**	**1.98%**
Late fee	$15			Acquisition cost	500,000	0.73%
Cost of funds	5%			Provision for loan loss	3,420,000	5.00%
Processing expense	$16.00			**Total expense**	**9,301,360**	**13.60%**
Servicing expense				Pre-tax profit	1,862,540	2.72%
per-call charge, per minute	$0.28			Taxes @40%	745,016	
early-stage collections, per year	$72			**Net income**	**1,117,524**	**1.63%**
late-stage collections, per year	$150			**Expense per active account**		
settlement & accounting, per year	$35,000			Processing	$16.00	
Provision for loan loss	5%			Servicing	$35.61	

CONTRASTING SERVICING EXPENSE

As we have noted earlier, one of the more significant differences between prime and subprime card portfolios is the service intensity and the attendant cost. By comparing the number of phone calls taken in the subprime portfolio per account, per year (approximately 10) versus the prime portfolio (approximately two) the first significant cost difference is apparent. The cost differential is further exacerbated by the average call length (subprime = 3 minutes, prime = 2 minutes). The other very significant difference is the collection expense. In the secured card program, collection expense is equal to 6.14% of average outstanding receivables, whereas in the unsecured program collection expense is equal to approximately 1.25% of receivables.

CONTRASTING INTEREST REVENUE

While interest revenue is an important driver in both the secured and unsecured portfolios, interest comprises a much larger portion of the overall revenue in the unsecured portfolio. That is, in the secured card program interest represents approximately 41% of total revenue whereas in the unsecured program it represents 72%. This relationship exists because the subprime arena is still largely fee-driven while the prime credit card business is in large part a "no fee" business. The interest spread in the secured card portfolio is, however, much larger than the spread in the unsecured business for two reasons: (1) there is little sensitivity to the APR and deposit rates, and (2) there is a much higher propensity to revolve balances.

CONTRASTING FEE REVENUE

The subprime credit card business subsists largely on fees. Even though the interest spread is very large (15.7% in our example) because the balances are low, the operational costs would make the cost of doing business prohibitive absent fees. Similarly, interchange revenue is not very meaningful in the subprime business since there is generally much lower spending. Most subprime issuers also generate a whopping component of their overall revenue through miscellaneous fees such as late fees, overlimit fees, NSF fees, etc.). In our hypothetical case, late fee revenue amounted to over 15% of the average outstanding portfolio balance! (To keep this in perspective, because the average balance is only $400, this equates to an average of three late charges per account.)

Beyond the composition of revenue and the varying impact of the operating expenses, the other major difference is the provision for loan losses. Subprime cards have a much higher loss rate (that is, incident rate) and the actual principal chargeoff amount is a function of many components including average balance, the lender/servicer's ability to keep overlimit amounts down, and the accounting treatment employed during chargeoff of accounts. On this last point, in the example above, we have shown the chargeoff amount as the gross amount of loss. Alternatively, many issuers reverse interest and fees out of revenue and charge off only the principal amount. The pre-tax profit is the same in either case, but one method overstates losses and the other overstates revenues. Although there is not clear unanimity of the treatment, most issuers reverse fees and interest on chargeoff and write off the principal balance.

SERVICING SUBPRIME CREDIT CARDS

Establishing Customer Service Levels

Most issuers adopt service-level standards that they believe are appropriate to their institution. If a prime card issuer decides to offer a subprime card, they may have a strong institutional bias toward extending comparable service levels to their subprime cardholders. This is not an economic decision but, rather, a philosophical business decision. Specialty subprime issuers, on the other hand, generally try to keep the servicing cost to a budgeted amount and let that determine service standards. For example, a subprime issuer may conclude that its cardholders will have to live with a lesser standard of convenience, and decide to only offer customer service during traditional business hours rather than seven days a week, 24 hours a day. The subprime issuer may also conclude that it is not imperative to answer each phone call within 20 seconds and that, in fact, their customers will "tolerate" a 60-second ASA. Taken to the furthest extreme, some subprime issuers will not offer an 800 number — as a means of further discouraging unnecessary phone contact.

Modifying Customer Behavior

Since the goal of both prime and subprime issuers is to generate a profit, both issuers wish to encourage many similar behaviors in their cardholders. For the prime issuer, these behaviors are primarily revenue-driven: spend more, revolve more and transfer balances to the card. For the subprime issuer, these same behaviors are also important but, since credit risk is the overarching concern, the other behavior that they must shape is payment behavior. This is done mainly through a very focused, soft early collection effort. It is very important to reach the customer early, to remind the customer of the payment obligation, and then to make it easy for the customer to comply.

Subprime issuers need to offer as many payment options and vehicles as possible, including money wire services and "pay by phone" bank draft services. In addition to the educational aspect to the customer contact, the consumer behavior is also shaped by the "stick" of penalty pricing. As we discussed in the P&L example, late fees are often a substantial penalty to a subprime customer. Many issuers also use "adaptive control" techniques and strategies to let the consumer's past behavior guide and influence the issuer's actions toward the cardholder. For example, a cardholder's past performance can be "learned" by a neural network model and used to influence numerous servicing actions such as:

Chapter 5: Credit Card Servicing for the Subprime Market

- Should this purchase by authorized?
- Should a collector call on a specific day, or at a specific stage of delinquency?
- Should a payment be treated normally, or should there be a "hold" on the available credit until the payment can be cleared?
- Should a card be reissued at expiration?

PROTECTING THE BANK

In the final analysis, the subprime credit card business is the recycling of the consumer's cash. In the secured card world, the recycling is generally explicit and obvious. In the case of the high-risk unsecured card, the recycling is less obvious but nonetheless present. The main idea is that until the consumer can demonstrate to the bank an acceptable level of creditworthiness, the bank must minimize its exposure to unsecured lending. This means developing systems to insure that overlimit transactions are minimized, payment postings do not make credit available in advance of cleared funds, delinquent customers are contacted promptly, and that the credit lines are treated very conservatively. The subprime credit card is first an access device and secondarily a loan.

Adrian Katz is vice chairman, chief operating officer, and chief financial officer of AutoBond Acceptance Corporation.

Katz has been involved in consumer finance since 1985 as a leader in the sale and financing through securitization of consumer assets. He joined AutoBond in November 1995 from Smith Barney, where he was a managing director responsible for structuring new asset-backed, commercial, and residential mortgage-backed securities.

From 1989 through 1994 he was at Prudential Securities where he worked as a managing director and co-head of the mortgage and asset capital division with sales, trading, banking, and research management responsibilities. He worked for the First Boston Corporation from 1985 to 1989 developing software and managing the structuring of new securitizations.

During his tenure in the securities industry Katz operated with Series 3, 7, 24, and 63 registrations. He has written much published research, including chapter 23 in the *Handbook of Mortgage Backed Securities*, published in 1992 by Probus Publishing Co., and chapter 18 in *The New High Yield Bond Market*, published in 1993 by Probus. He has chaired and spoken at numerous industry conferences.

Katz holds a B.S.E. in electrical engineering and computer science from Princeton University.

Chapter 6

Subprime Automobile Financing

Adrian Katz
Vice Chairman, Chief Operating Officer,
and Chief Financial Officer
AutoBond Acceptance Corporation

The development of the subprime automobile finance industry has resembled a sometimes reckless ride on a rickety Coney Island roller coaster. However, despite the current wobbly legs of a baby, this industry will mature and emerge as a developed and important consumer finance sector in the United States.

There are approximately $600 billion of sales of automobiles each year. For consumers, car expenditures represent the second-largest component of their budget, second only to housing. Estimates vary, but it is generally believed that about 40% of American consumers have some form of credit impairment that could prevent them from obtaining prime automobile financing. In the past few years, the average new vehicle purchase price has exceeded the average American annual wage, and this has resulted in an increased need for consumer financing and an increase in used vehicle sales. Given that almost all vehicle purchases involve some form of financing, the figures suggest that the annual subprime automobile finance activity could exceed $200 billion.

HISTORY

Due to the commercial opportunities implicit in the sheer prospective size of the subprime automobile finance market, the industry was compelled to develop. There are two key areas of risk inherent in providing financing in this sector. The first is credit assessment involving the customer's capacity and inclination to make payments. The second type of risk involves the assessment of the automobile as collateral. Given an automobile dealer's general objective to move inventory and its position of best understanding the collateral, it is not surprising that the subprime automobile finance industry first emerged as a form of captive financing by the larger and better capitalized dealership groups.

Fueling the pressure for the expansion of subprime automobile financing has been the increased volume of used car sales. Used car sales have increased for several reasons, including:

- The rise of vehicle leasing as a financing method for almost one out of three new vehicles and the resulting constant supply of cars rolling off leases after a few years.
- The improvements in vehicle manufacture resulting in reduced maintenance expenses and increased vehicle longevity.
- The aforementioned rise in the past few years of new vehicle prices exceeding the average American wage, resulting in increased consumer activity in the more affordable used car market.

There is a chicken-and-egg aspect to the increase in used-car sales with respect to subprime financing in that the very availability of financing has also increased used-car sales.

Used cars are sold by both new-vehicle franchised dealers (approximately 22,000 nationwide) and independent used-vehicle dealers (approximately 78,000 nationwide). The franchised dealers typically have had better access to financing for the development of their in-house subprime financing activities, while the independent dealers typically have had more of their customers with subprime credit profiles.

Certain geographic parts of the country were hotbeds for the development of the subprime automobile finance industry, reflective of economic realities in the respective regions. For example, Texas underwent in some respects a depressionlike economic period in the 1980s due to the combined effects of a decline in energy prices, the burst of a real estate bubble, and the failure of many financial institutions. Many Texans experienced damaged credit as a result of this rough period and, for several years, Texas car dealers were unable to obtain vehicle financing for their average customer. By necessity, many Texas car dealers developed in-house subprime financing capabilities to address their local realities. Some of the legacy of this history can be observed in the fact that today there are a disproportionate number of subprime finance companies based in Texas.

The early subprime financing activities at dealerships are important because these dealerships proved to be the training ground for much of the management talent that participated in the subsequent development of the subprime automobile finance companies that are now driving the industry. The reasons for the subprime automobile finance industry to develop beyond the efforts of dealers include:

- Needed access to capital on a larger scale.
- Diversification of risks.
- Organizational conflicts between pressures to sell and rational credit-decisioning.

Even large dealer groups do not have enough volume of subprime customer sales to have the economies of scale to compete effectively through in-house financing. The past provides lessons of dealer groups that have failed to be successful at both selling and financing vehicles, with the most notable being URCARCO, today reorganized as Americredit and solely involved in subprime financing.

Other early entrants into the arena of subprime automobile financing include large finance companies involved for many years in financing automobile dealers and customers with prime credit profiles; with time, they have migrated further out on the credit risk branch to include weaker subprime customers. The earliest successful entrant into the automobile finance industry with essentially one-dimensional intentions to serve the subprime sector was Mercury Finance in the 1980s. It was not until the 1990s that competition broadened into the industry we observe today, with about 25 public companies and numerous private entities.

UNDERWRITING

Tiering

The market for subprime automobile financing is by no means homogenous. There are varieties of niches with different nomenclature and attributes. In general, customer credits are delineated as either A, B, C, or D credits. The A credit customers are what are generally considered prime and will be provided financing by captive finance companies such as GMAC or banking institutions such as Chase Bank. The subprime industry has a significant involvement in the so-called A-minus credit sector, although this categorization is probably euphemistic and such credits are essentially B credits. From time to time, traditional prime funding sources have been observed participating in the B credit sector, although they would probably not admit as such. B credit customers will have some relatively minor blemish on their credit record but will generally evidence a willingness and capacity to make finance payments. The C credits represent the most typical profile of subprime customer and this would involve someone who has experienced a tangible credit problem while also evidencing a viability to make payments. The D credits are generally representative of such chronic borrowers that the few companies active at this end of the spectrum resemble collection agencies with heavy reliance on the financing structure and collateral recoverability. Casual observers should not place much faith in the credit-profile representations of industry participants.

Technology/Scoring

Consistent with the development cycles in other consumer lending, the subprime automobile financing industry is developing an increasing utilization of statistically driven credit scoring models for pricing and/or underwriting determinations. There are financial services companies (such as Fair Isaac) that specialize in offering scoring products to the industry, while market participants have also developed in-house scoring models. Scoring models generally are most effective in determining whether a prospective customer is a prime or subprime borrower, and such models are usually less insightful with respect to the gradients within the subprime realm. However, scoring models are an especially useful tool for originators as a pricing guide and can assist the processing of large application volume more efficiently. For example, scoring models can broadly categorize applications for credit underwriters as either unacceptable, worthy of more detailed analysis, or strong candidates.

For scoring models to be effective, the originator is best served by building such models on a foundation of extensive and reliable underwriting and collection data. Some industry participants do not have track records over long-enough periods of time, while others have not retained sufficient finance contract and performance-level detail for the optimal development of scoring models. At this writing, scoring models are primarily for internal use at subprime finance companies but, with time and progress, it is plausible that scoring model results will in some way be communicated to equity and debt investors.

DEFAULTS

The most critical risk factor for analysis by industry operating management, investors, equity analysts, and rating agencies is that of the default rates experienced and projected. The frequency of default and, to a lesser extent, the associated loss severity, dominate the success or failure equation. Defaults are measured via several methodologies including:

- A cumulative rate since the inception of a portfolio.
- A current rate for the most recent reporting period (typically monthly for securitization servicing and quarterly for SEC disclosures).

- The generally most informative format of a static pool presentation involving time-dimensional vectors.

Various sources of information, including public companies and research analysts, suggest that default rates are generally lower initially with increases experienced through the first year of seasoning, peaking from about a year to a year and a half of seasoning, and, thereafter, data evidences steady declines as shown in Exhibit 1.

Exhibit 1: Typical Static Pool Default Curve

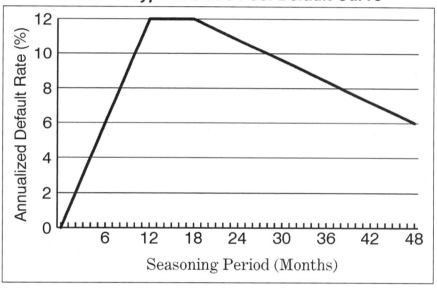

The typical static pool curve correlates with the following behavioral scenario:

- Initial default rates are usually low as obligor credit is recently reviewed and deemed acceptable in the underwriting process. Therefore, borrowers should exhibit a capacity to pay initially. An exception to this scenario is for a pool that is poorly underwritten and/or not adequately verified.
- Credit difficulties for subprime obligors arise with time and, on average, peak after about a year, indicating such influences as their average time to become unemployed, depletion of savings if any, and/or too many incremental subsequent credit burdens.
- Obligors that manage to make payments as many as 18 times

apparently have the inclination, the perception, and, possibly, the reality of built-up equity in their loan, and the wherewithal to continue to make payments. There is evidenced continued credit improvement through time as a finance contract pool reaches maturity. Incidentally, given typical finance contract advance amounts (initial loan-to-value ratios) in the subprime automobile finance industry, an obligor might need to make as much as three years of payments before effectively building up equity in the loan. With time a given static pool has adverse deselection in that obligors surviving in a pool are on average better than those that have literally defaulted out of the pool.

Default rates are generally high for subprime automobile finance contracts and cumulative rates typically range from 15% to as much as 40%. However, for a business plan to be successful it is the interrelationship of pricing and default rates that matters. Valid business plans can operate at the higher end of the default range subject to appropriate pricing while, conversely, a company may fail with lower default rates if its pricing algorithm does not provide sufficient profit margin.

Default outcomes are not only impacted by underwriting standards but can be driven higher through insufficient verification and funding discipline as well as weak servicing. Several industry participants have appropriate written underwriting guidelines and yet have either permitted too many exceptions, failed to determine the accuracy of applicant information integral to the credit decision, and/or have operated with infrastructure too weak to support vigorous collections and asset disposition.

RECOVERIES

Unlike mortgage lending, in which there is no difficulty finding the asset securing a loan in the event of default, the subprime automobile finance contract collateral is literally on wheels. This mobility suggests risks and nuances to the recovery process. Further, recoveries frequently include insurance claim proceeds (from both primary obligor and possibly vendor's single interest (VSI)/deficiency balance policies) and soft-add product refunds such as from warranties. The intensity of the collection and asset disposition process for subprime automobile finance contracts exceeds that applied to many other types of credit customers and collateral types, and must involve sufficiently skilled personnel and technology capabilities.

Recovery strategies vary across the industry, such as with

respect to the optimal approach to selling repossessed vehicles — via wholesale at auction or by some form of retail remarketing. The industry typically achieves recoveries of approximately half of the outstanding finance contract amount from vehicle sale proceeds. This sales/proceeds recovery ratio is much influenced by the original loan-to-value financing advance amount and the equipment verification process up front. Initial loan-to-value advance ratios greatly impact the ultimate loss severity and therefore the collateral value should not be permitted to be too unrelated to the loan amount.

Some industry participants pursue self-insured strategies to enhance ultimate recoveries while others have purchased VSI insurance (collateral protection), and deficiency balance insurance (credit default coverage). All obligors are supposed to maintain certain minimum insurance as dictated by applicable laws; however, given that such insurance is often not maintained by weaker credit customers, it is relatively common for VSI insurance to be obtained by finance companies. There have been several instances of apparent reneging by VSI/deficiency insurance providers, notwithstanding the fact that several industry participants purchased such policies. There has been a decline in their perceived added value on the part of investors, rating agencies, and the industry itself.

Soft-add products are usually financed by the subprime automobile finance companies. Hence, the portion of the soft-add premium paid for but implicitly not used due to a premature maturity associated with a default event is, in most instances, eligible for refund. Given the old adage that time is money, a final important element in the economics of recoveries is the extent of any delay in realizing cash proceeds.

PREPAYMENTS

Unlike mortgage-related consumer assets, there is essentially no interest rate-motivated refinancing activity with respect to subprime automobile finance contracts. The typical subprime automobile finance contract is fairly short in cash-flow duration, usually less than two years, and therefore is less profitable for refinancing consideration and the consequences of a refinancing for an obligor or an investor are minimal. The majority of prepayments are associated with vehicle trade-in transactions. Very rarely does a subprime credit customer have sufficient funds to prepay arbitrarily from savings for the sole purpose of extinguishing his or her liability. Various sources of data suggest that prepayments in the subprime automobile sector range from about 0.5% to 1.0% per month (6% to 12% annually) and are fairly consistent throughout the life of a pool of finance contracts. The very first month or so of seasoning can be a statistical anomaly in that prepayments can result from customers returning vehicles to dealerships due to some type of dissatisfaction.

OBLIGOR AND CONTRACT PROFILE

The typical borrower is more like the average American than might be first assumed. The average age is in the mid-30s, the average income bracket is $25,000 to $35,000, and most demonstrate at least a year of employment and residency time. The typical range of monthly subprime automobile finance contract payment amounts is $250 to $400, and the implied cost-of-funds penalty (due to higher interest rates) versus a prime borrower's comparable obligation is about $50 to $100 per month. Amounts financed range substantially but generally average less than $10,000. Coupon rates range substantially (and are constrained in several states by local usury law) but generally average about 20%. Payment terms rarely extend beyond five years and — through defaults, prepayments, and amortization — a typical pool of finance contracts will have an average life of approximately two years and a cash flow duration of less than two years. Some finance contracts are structured as "Rule of 78s," while the majority are level payment and self-amortizing.

INDUSTRY PROBLEMS

The early market leader, Mercury Finance, and many to follow, would ultimately experience demise through such factors as fraud, miscalculation, judgment errors, irresponsible competition, uncontrolled growth, and lack of continued access to capital. The industry remains in turmoil and transition, and a discussion of the industry difficulties is worthwhile.

Illiquidity

Market conditions with respect to liquidity availability in the subprime automobile finance industry have dramatically changed course. The intuitive appeal of the profit potential in this industry assisted the rapid formation of capital in the early 1990s. High subprime automobile finance contract coupons coupled with acquisition fees and the potential scale of the market seemed a certain bet to many investors. However, the majority of enterprises garnering capital in the early 1990s were essentially unproven and many were not much more than a few people with business plans. The initial public offering (IPO) environment was constructive at that time, and large financial institutions provided leveraged capital through warehouse and securitization investment activities.

In the late 1990s, capital conditions changed markedly. The first break in the dike occurred in early 1997 with the unfolding story of alleged fraud and losses at the perceived market leader, Mercury Finance. Prior to 1997, many companies successfully raised capital by presenting their business strategies in the context and by comparison with the apparent success of Mercury Finance; therefore, its failure was very adversely significant. Throughout 1997 and 1998 additional industry participants encountered headwinds and some failed in part due to their lack of access to financial liquidity. Invariably, liquidity was denied to the companies with intrinsic flaws in their business models. However, with the sheer number of corporate bankruptcies at this time, even subprime automobile finance companies with capable management and viable business models have found capital formation extremely difficult.

Too Rapid Growth

As capital was formed, many burgeoning companies deployed such capital too rapidly. There are many factors that led to excessive growth rates and resulting adverse consequences. To the extent capital was raised through the IPO process, management at most companies experienced significant pressure from investors and research analysts to produce ever-increasing quarterly profits through ever-increasing acquisition volume. Additionally, management of several companies was often undisciplined in their enthusiasm and did not, in parallel to their acquisition growth, develop commensurate infrastructure to support their operations. Technology implementation and personnel hiring and training often lagged with disastrous consequences.

Not only did rapid growth impact the operational requirements for many companies but, depending on the financial leveraging of the involved company, it often entailed an increasing need for incremental capital. Access to capital, volume driving revenue and profits, and growth driving the need for additional capital became a treadmill for many — with unintended and damaging consequences. Ironically, the current profit potential of the subprime automobile finance industry is more compelling for surviving companies with the patience necessary to build a successful business, due to the failures and thinning of the competitive landscape by those participants that grew too rapidly.

Credit Quality

There are many credit niches within the general category of subprime. Business models can work for different credit gradients subject to the appropriate pricing and adequate servicing support. With relatively insufficient historical experience, several companies did not design their underwriting credit criteria and pricing matrices to generate viable profit outcomes. In a number of instances companies developed workable credit and price objectives and yet did not employ the necessary discipline to enforce their criteria. Some companies have excellent underwriting guidelines but their portfolios are riddled with exceptions. Even if finance contracts are acquired with discipline and viable criteria, the ability to collect and — when necessary — perform asset disposition, is also crucial to profitable outcomes. Poor credit quality is usually intertwined with too rapid growth and/or inadequate infrastructure.

Third-Party Servicing

The intensity necessary to perform subprime automobile finance servicing is often the difference between success and failure. Companies with retained economic interests in their financing activities, such as excess spread retention in a securitization, usually possess the upside motivation to perform effectively as servicer. Third-party servicing usually involves relatively disinterested service providers with cost-control incentives and no upside maximization motivation. The appeal to many originators with respect to third-party servicing is that it permits a young company to focus on finance contract acquisitions and related infrastructure support while relying on an existing servicing platform not requiring investment. In the formative years of the industry there was much appeal to the deep-pocketed, third-party servicing participants but, with more recent experience, that rose has lost much of its bloom. Back-up servicing has become a more popular mechanism with investors and rating agencies for addressing any concerns regarding the financial staying power of an issuer/servicer in a securitization.

Asset Dispositions

There are different asset disposition strategies pursued in the subprime automobile finance industry. Some companies have attempted to be integrated to the extent that they have actually owned retail lots to facilitate the sale of repossessed vehicles. Other companies have taken the philosophical approach that they are finance companies and, hence, all asset disposition activities are conducted on a wholesale basis through auction. These companies take the perspective that automobiles are depreciating and noninterest-earning assets and, therefore, should be sold as quickly as possible. There is much debate regarding the efficacy of each asset disposition approach, but it is the general view that finance companies are making a mistake to the extent that they attempt to retail remarket repossessions. Some observers believe that the retailing of repossessed vehicles was an attempt to obfuscate and defer losses by some industry participants when their projected recovery rates were not achieved.

ACCOUNTING

Accounting challenges that exist in the subprime automobile finance industry include aggressive gain-on-sale treatment under Generally Accepted Accounting Principles (GAAP), fraud, and inconsistent accounting treatment.

Aggressive GAAP Gain-on-Sale

Some of the accounting difficulties are accentuated by the accounting methodology of reflecting, as a GAAP income contribution, the value of retained assets formed when a sale event, typically a securitization, is transacted. Implicit in such income recognition are numerous assumptions and therein lies the risk of aggressive GAAP gain-on-sale. In several instances, a lack of historical experience coupled with natural optimism caused erroneous accounting assumptions to be employed; this, in turn, resulted in inaccurate forecasting of future cash flow and valuation. In some instances, knowing fraud was perpetrated by the use of invalid forecasting.

The equity represented on the balance sheet of many companies in the subprime automobile finance industry is typically volatile, in large part due to the inherently leveraged retained interests and their related GAAP gain-on-sale treatment. The accounting profession and subprime automobile finance industry management experienced much pressure during 1998 to bring assumptions into line with realistic expectations, and this has resulted in some fairly large recent earnings restatements. Current GAAP gain-on-sale determinations and retained asset valuations are generally fairly presented across the subprime automobile finance industry. Given some of the vociferous criticisms of gain-on-sale accounting treatment, it is noteworthy that the largest bankruptcy in the subprime automobile finance industry involved Mercury Finance, a company that did not engage in securitization sales and therefore did not have any application of gain-on-sale accounting.

Fraud

Fraud is a risk that exists in all industries to some extent. Contrary to the emphasis of certain jaded observers, fraud is not endemic to the subprime automobile finance industry. However, fraud can be more difficult to detect in industries involving financial assets where the assets are "on paper" as opposed to being visibly tangible. Entering 1999, there are instances of alleged fraud in the industry but no related convictions or confirming conclusive civil litigation. Fraud has been alleged but not proven as of yearend 1998 with respect to Mercury Finance and First Merchants Acceptance.

Inconsistent Accounting

As is often the case with evolving industries, there is a tendency to have fragmented opinions on how to best represent assets on a balance sheet and how appropriately to record income. Some of the accounting inconsistencies that exist are not necessarily as a result of nefarious intentions on the part of market participants and/or their accountants. Instances exist of accounting firms advising certain treatments to one company while, in a different part of the country, providing different advice. Similar inconsistent feedback has been widely discussed with respect to the Securities and Exchange Commission (SEC).

There is no single interpretive accounting authority for all issues, and this has caused difficulties for all interested parties — especially the investment community. Examples of inconsistencies would include the relatively simple choice of discount rate for present value calculations and the more complicated aspects of the appropriate amount of disaggregation in the balance-sheet presentation of retained interests. Some equity analysts have recently complained to the Financial Accounting Standards Board (FASB) that GAAP gain-on-sale accounting treatment has been misleading as implemented and is causing valuation errors in their research publications. In early 1999 FASB was floating a proposal to address some of these presentation and assumption issues. Aspects of this complaint involve excuses for earnings projection errors, while there is merit to some of the criticism associated with gain-on-sale accounting.

OPERATIONAL CONSIDERATIONS

Most subprime automobile finance companies are structured and legally registered as consumer finance companies. This is an important distinction with respect to the common misunderstanding that the majority of these companies perform as lenders.

Pricing

There is important operating and pricing flexibility associated with being a consumer finance company versus a lender, most notably, the ability to acquire finance contracts at a price other than par, typically at a discount. Purchase discounts range from as much as 20% to zero, although discounts on average are probably less than 10%. Some finance contract acquisitions involve the automobile dealer retaining risk in the form of credit performance recourse. This recourse-acquisition structure is more common with finance contracts in the weakest D credit sector. Credit Acceptance Corporation would be an example of a company employing recourse-acquisition structures.

Marketing

In general, subprime finance companies do not initiate customers through traditional retail-oriented marketing. Typically, automobile dealers screen customers through dialogue and a review of their credit history prior to directing their application for consideration to various finance companies. These customers usually enter into a conditional sales contract with the automobile dealer and may be permitted to take possession of the vehicle prior to the completion of the sale of the contract to the ultimate finance company. The costs of attracting subprime automobile finance customers therefore typically more approximate wholesale as opposed to retail origination platforms. Subprime automobile finance companies mostly market their services directly to automobile dealerships rather than individuals.

Infrastructure

Subprime finance companies usually have two fairly distinct divisions, their origination platforms and a servicing infrastructure. Feedback between the two is very important in that collection experience can and should influence underwriting criteria and practice.

ORIGINATION PLATFORMS

The origination platforms are usually divided into marketing, loan underwriting, verification, and funding. Marketing primarily generates and maintains relationships with automobile dealers. Loan underwriters review applications and determine their creditworthiness while interacting with their finance and insurance (F&I) counterparties at the dealerships. Such interactions, by fax and telephone, would often include conveying any applicable stipulations, paperwork required, and verification procedures. Verification and funding professionals usually review all aspects of a given finance contract and accompanying materials before a check is issued to consummate a purchase.

A significant factor influencing the relative costs of operation across subprime automobile finance companies is the presence of regional offices, if any. With the relentless progress of technology and communication tools, there is no longer the need for origination platforms to operate on a local level. There are strong arguments — both the incremental bricks-and-mortar expense and the lack of direct, more closely monitored, credit control — suggesting that the branch network business model is suboptimal. Conversely, there are industry participants who contend that there are intangible benefits to closer customer proximity.

SERVICING

The servicing infrastructure is usually divided into collections (which in turn is often further divided by delinquency status), repossession activities, vehicle sales, insurance recoveries, soft-add recoveries, and investor reporting. The collection personnel spend much of their time contacting obligors and reminding them of their delinquency status and encouraging them to make payments. Aspects of the collection process are humanly intensive while technology tools such as predictive dialers and efficient database software can be very helpful.

The vehicle repossession function is usually not performed by employees of subprime automobile finance companies but, instead, is subcontracted to bonded agents specialized in such activities. There are skills and risks unique to the repossession profession. Skip tracing is sometimes necessary and usually performed by a specialized servicing professional. Vehicle dispositions involve specifically expert personnel who would either process vehicles through wholesale auctions and/or retail remarket vehicles directly to retail customers. Direct experience selling automobiles is a must for the vehicle disposition role.

Insurance claim processing is typically a detailed and demanding task of paperwork and tenacity and, invariably, specialists perform these functions.

Given the very intensive nature of the various servicing functions, employee incentives and goal-oriented management are necessary for best results. Servicing departments and, especially, third-party servicers sometimes fail in large part due to the lack of such efforts to align and motivate personnel toward definable outcomes.

Significant investment in technology is required to support an effective servicing operation: database software to store and retrieve obligor information interactively, software to process customer payments and any account postings, software to organize and prioritize customer calling teams, software to monitor and report on detailed and statistical performance characteristics, predictive dialers, network and server equipment, computers for almost all personnel, in-house technology professionals, and adequate personnel training.

Investor Reporting

Investor reporting capabilities can prove critical to the continued success of a subprime automobile finance company in that access to capital is often interwoven with investor information and confidence. For public companies, investor reporting can extend beyond administration reporting for a particular bond issue to include SEC filings, such as Form 10-Q and Form 10-K. In hindsight, many investor reporting templates negotiated at the time transactions were issued have not proven adequate for investor risk assessment and ongoing comfort. Periodic accounting procedures letters can often provide support to the efforts of issuing and servicing companies with respect to investor reporting.

CAPITAL FORMATION

The success or failure of a finance company active in any asset category, especially the troubled subprime automobile finance industry, depends greatly on its capital structure. Financial market conditions are at times (including 1999 and the foreseeable future) in flux while continuous access to capital and/or sufficient capital liquidity reserves for adverse environments is a necessity. Capital is needed for operational expenses, financing during collateral accumulation and retention of interests in securitizations.

Operating Capital

Equity Usually, the scarcest and most expensive form of capital is equity, both common and preferred. Sources of equity capital supporting the subprime automobile finance industry include SEC-registered stock offerings to the general public (both IPOs and secondary offerings), private placements with institutional or qualifying retail investors, and investments by entrepreneurial management. Currently, there is little likelihood of access to either the IPO or public secondary market for even the best subprime automobile finance companies, given existing market perceptions. This author is unaware of any successful common stock offering within the subprime automobile finance industry in 1998. Stock price performance for subprime automobile finance companies in the past year has been dismal which, in turn, undermines any new equity capital-raising initiatives, as shown in Exhibit 2.

Similar to debt in many regards, preferred equity is a form of equity that has credit preference relative to common stock and usually pays a tangible dividend. Preferred stock has certain consequences for corporate income as would any interest payment on debt, but is not as

Exhibit 2: Selected Stock Price Performance for Publicly Traded Subprime Automobile Finance Companies During 1998

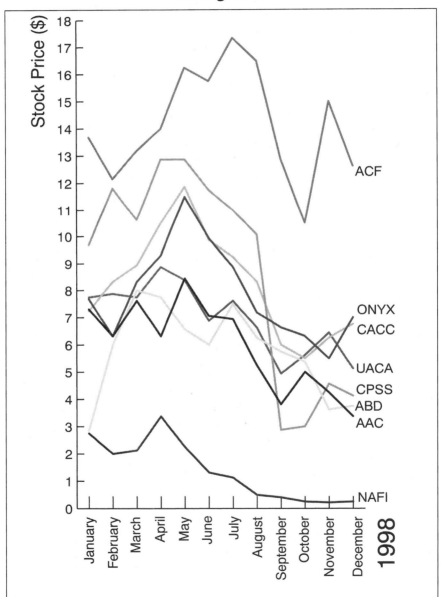

dilutive as common stock. Preferred stock does have certain special tax characteristics. This author's company, AutoBond Acceptance Corporation, issued SEC registered preferred stock in 1998 and therefore evidenced the viability at that time of this type of capital formation. The benefit of all common equity and most preferred equity is that the issuing subprime automobile finance company is not usually required to pay back the proceeds to investors at any time and such capital is therefore categorized as permanent capital.

In the early to mid-1990s there was an active equity market with many investment banks vying for equity underwriting and ancillary business opportunities within the emerging subprime automobile finance industry. Important considerations for companies considering accessing the public capital markets included the sales distribution capabilities and the equity research and publishing reputations of the various investment banking companies. With the relatively recent collapse of several industry participants there has been a vacuum of research published and expertise available for investors.

Many investment banks have recently deemed the subprime automobile finance industry an unprofitable sector for their services and have dropped their secondary market support (including market-making trading activities) with compounding consequences to an industry already under siege. Inherent in an environment of a lack of analysis, information, and liquidity are investment opportunities for the educated risk-taker. Some investors hold the view that the current disarray of the public equity market presents significant opportunity.

Private placement investing thrived alongside the active public market during the early to mid-1990s. Most private equity investors gained comfort and courage from the apparent liquidity and exit strategy implicitly available to them through the public offering market during this time. With the recent public market activity demise, so, too, has the private placement market suffered. However, there have emerged bottom-fishing contrarian private placement investors seeking value in special distressed situations. These companies, in most instances expert in finance and having access to tangible capital, are intrigued by the challenges and opportunities inherent in adverse conditions. Some recent private equity investments have come from investors already embroiled in the subprime automobile finance industry deploying additional capital to shore up existing commitments.

Debt The raising of capital through the placement of debt is currently viable for subprime automobile finance companies. The debt market is by no means liquid and transactions are very much by appointment but, nonetheless, placements are active. Almost all such placements involve some form of equity sweetener to induce the bond investor. In a sense, debt investors are currently achieving some equitylike upside while securing a priority credit position in the capital structure of an issuer. These debt instruments are usually in the form of convertible debt or debt with warrants attached. A recent such issuer was Consumer Portfolio Services. Many of the investors involved in these hybrid forms of debt are not necessarily focused or expert on the subprime automobile finance industry but are expert at financial structuring and believe that they can build adequate downside protection into their investment strategies within the industry. For many issuers the appeal of debt is that this form of capital is generally less dilutive with respect to earnings per share. Conversely, debt ultimately must be repaid at maturity and even interest payments reduce available operating cash flow.

Warehousing

Securitization activity, the ultimate risk and asset deconsolidation strategy for most subprime automobile finance companies, requires the process of sufficient asset accumulation for the formation of a statistically diverse pool and the necessary economies of scale for an efficient cost of funds. Warehouse financing arrangements are a critical component of the process. Warehouse financing is provided to the industry by a wide range of companies including commercial banks, investment banks, insurance companies, and finance companies.

Commercial banks were very active in providing warehousing to the industry in the early to mid-1990s through on-balance-sheet funding structures. However, with the more recent difficulties in the subprime automobile finance companies the commercial banks have been quick to withdraw their support. Some would argue that they have actually unduly precipitated problems through their nervous haste to retreat.

Investment banks have generally provided warehousing in connection with obtaining corollary mandates to underwrite the resulting securitizations. Such investment banking-linked interim financing facilities have usually proved cheaper sources of capital for subprime automobile finance companies than alternatives, as the applicable investment bank has been predominantly motivated by underwriting fees. Further, investment banks have usually provided more cash advances against collateral (a very appealing feature) to subprime automobile finance companies than to traditionally more conservative participants such as commercial banks.

The participation by insurance companies in providing warehousing capital has generally been through investments in investment-grade structured warehouse trusts. Such facilities are typically designed with some form of credit enhancement and bankruptcy-remote borrowing vehicle more akin to a variable-rate and variable-sized securitization. Capital requirements imposed by the National Association of Insurance Commissioners (NAIC) have usually influenced the structure and, in particular, the rating objectives of the involved insurance companies.

Commercial paper (CP) conduits have emerged as important sources of interim capital for the industry. Most of the CP conduits require liquidity and/or credit enhancement features to accommodate subprime automobile finance contracts as eligible collateral. Almost all CP conduits can accept subprime automobile finance contracts as a part of a diversified asset base. However, they usually have exposure limitations and may not choose to participate in the industry.

Finance company participation is as varied as the lenders but includes such large and influential players as GE Capital, real estate investment trusts (REITs), and some relatively unknown specialty finance companies. Finance company lenders are typically characterized as collateral-based lenders and are generally known to offer their funds at relatively higher rates.

Whatever the interim financing source, a successful business plan in the subprime automobile finance industry must entail supportive warehouse funding arrangements.

Securitization

Ultimately, even the best capitalized subprime automobile finance companies will find it necessary to access the capital markets through the securitization of finance contracts. There are many structures, objectives, and involved participants in the securitization process. Participants may include underwriters, servicers, rating agents, investors, insurers, trustees, lawyers, and accountants.

Current market conditions favor structures that are bond-insured such that investors have enhanced credit comfort through the presence of a knowledgeable and protecting intermediary. Financial Security Assurance (FSA) is the most active monoline bond insurance company in the subprime automobile finance sector. Even in past years when subprime automobile finance companies were held in better regard, there was an investor bias toward enhanced transactions. However, this structural approach has come at a relatively high price to the liquidity of several issuers, in that performance triggers integrated in the bond indentures and monoline enhancement agreements have frequently been tripped, causing excess cash flow in these issuances to be trapped as incremental self-enhancement.

In light of the current liquidity constraints endemic in the subprime automobile finance industry, the biggest influence on structuring is the goal of maximizing the amount of monetization realized by an issuer up front. This is achieved through efforts to maximize the percent of a transaction that is investment grade and therefore more marketable, and by the solicitation of the sparse audience of potential subordinate security investors. The rating agencies play a pivotal role in this process, and their apparent tendency towards increasing conservatism with respect to the subprime automobile finance companies has generally adversely impacted an issuers pursuit of optimal monetization.

Mistakes have been made in financial engineering since the first securitization of subprime automobile finance contracts, causing ongoing ramifications, while optimal structuring has not always proven protection for investors with respect to underperforming collateral. Problems have developed with third-party servicers taking fees but not performing per servicing agreements and with insurance companies providing VSI/deficiency balance coverage and refusing to pay claims either in full and/or in a timely fashion. However, investors in investment-grade securities have suffered relatively little in the way of actual financial damage to date despite certain problems. Subordinate investors have not faired nearly as well and some have lost much of their investment principal. Such adverse outcomes for subordinate investors have transpired in part due to collateral underperformance and due to the very structural features intended to protect senior bond investors and/or credit enhancers.

The yield spreads versus comparable Treasury bonds offered on subprime automobile finance contract collateralized securities widened substantially during much of 1998. Yield spreads on triple-A-rated securities widened by more than 1% to a current range of 1.7% to 2%. Investors are willing to participate in this sector but expect more for their perceived risk and liquidity concerns. Some subordinate securities may not currently be marketable at any yield spread. This yield spread widening during the second half of 1998 was in conjunction with broader capital market dislocations, and there is a reasonable expectation that yield spreads for subprime automobile finance contract collateralized securities will decrease as market turmoil subsides.

Mergers and Acquisitions

Due to operating adversities and significant challenges facing the subprime automobile finance companies there has been a significant increase in merger and acquisition activity. Ironically, the tough competition for capital within the industry has resulted in reduced competition for the acquisition of finance contracts. This environment, where many subprime automobile finance companies offer excellent operating platforms with a less competitive backdrop while being strapped for cash, is inherently intriguing to opportunistic acquirers. Several operating platforms are for sale at prices significantly less than the total dollars invested in their infrastructure development and potential franchise values. Others, despite being cheap, are worthless.

There has been relatively little consolidation within the industry of the type where a subprime automobile finance company purchases a competitor. However, there has been a form of consolidation in which numerous finance contract portfolios have been sold to stronger companies and/or personnel have been recruited from one industry participant to another. Generally, for an already operating company there is not much to be gained in efficiencies or relationships by buying an entire franchise from a competitor. However, for financial institutions such as commercial banks and consumer finance companies previously uninvolved in the subprime automobile finance industry, there can be much to gain from a strategic acquisition of a franchise complementary to existing lending activities. In addition to traditional merger-and-acquisition activities, various interim or hybrid forms of partnership arrangements have developed between subprime automobile finance companies and better-capitalized entities.

CONCLUSIONS

People will continue to buy automobiles. Many people will continue to need financing to assist their purchases of automobiles. Many people will continue to create blemished credit records for themselves. Many people will continue to need subprime automobile finance companies to provide acquisition financing. Dealers will continue to sell automobiles. Many dealers will continue to need subprime automobile finance companies to meet sales objectives and operate profitably.

Despite all of the current turmoil there are fundamental behavioral and economic reasons for confidence in the future of the subprime automobile finance industry. Capital formation and long-term profitability will prevail for the best companies through the maturation of a young industry. Subprime automobile finance will for the foreseeable future be a part of the consumer finance landscape. Financially affording and owning a vehicle — and enjoying its associated freedom to drive to work, go out on a date in the evening, and visit family on the weekend — is as American as apple pie.

Cliff Grubbs is the manager of the acquisitions and sourcing group for PRIMUS Automotive Financial Services, based in Nashville, Tennessee. PRIMUS is a division of Ford Motor Credit Company.

Grubbs joined PRIMUS in February 1994. He is responsible for the management of all phases of whole-loan/lease portfolio purchases and the marketing of flow-retail and lease-receivable origination programs to major banking institutions and independent finance companies.

PRIMUS provides private-label wholesale, retail, and lease financing for a number of automotive manufacturers including Jaguar, Mazda, Subaru, and Suzuki in the United States. PRIMUS also purchases retail and lease receivables from affiliated financial institution originators.

Prior to joining PRIMUS, Grubbs spent 10 years in the banking industry in senior lending and management positions with Guarantee Federal Savings Bank, Dallas, San Jacinto Savings, Houston, and Mbank Grand Prairie, all in Texas. During his tenure in the Texas banking industry, he developed expertise in asset generation, credit risk management, and the underwriting of secondary market transactions involving automotive and many other consumer loan products.

Grubbs received his bachelor's degree in business administration, in finance, from Texas Tech University.

Chapter 7

Subprime Auto Paper: Promised Land or Nightmare?

Cliff Grubs
Manager, Acquisitions Group
PRIMUS Automotive Financial Services

Many bankers wish they could shift gears, in automotive terms, to put recent events surrounding the subprime auto lending market in reverse.

Certain financial products seem to come full cycle every four or five years and create the expectation of unparalleled returns. In an epoch when most A auto receivables were earning minimal yields or getting gobbled up by the securitization types, subprime auto paper jumped to the top of the list in the resurgence of high-return investments. Those who have been in the field for at least the decade of the 1990s will recall that subprime paper had been at the top of this list before, and also at the bottom.

Subprime paper may retain a strong appeal entering the 21st century because the fundamentals exist for a sound investment program. However, when the personalities and ethics of investment bankers and auto dealers are combined with the desire of investors to earn big yields, "complications" are bound to occur. Let's examine the pros and cons of this type of investment.

ATTRACTIONS OF SUBPRIME LOANS

There are a number of significant factors — on paper, at least — supporting the profitability of subprime auto receivables.

- Lower-tier auto paper during the 1990s has been much like credit card receivables used to be. The rates often stay at the legal maximum (18% or higher) regardless of the interest rate environment at any given point. If your funding cost is 5% to 8%, you don't have to be a rocket scientist to determine you have some room for above-average credit losses.

- The automobile finance market is huge (15 million new vehicles plus over 30 million used vehicles on an annual basis.) There are enough paying customers at all credit levels to build a sizable portfolio.

- Tough economic times and middle-management downsizing in corporate America have left a lot of good, honest people with credit bureau records historically found only with lower-tier credits. These individuals should pay well if the economy continues to grow or if the Fed manages to orchestrate the much-talked-about "soft landing" that appears increasingly likely.

- Consumer loans by their very nature diversify risk and are relatively predictable. Even in lower-tier credit, losses can be predictable.

- Despite all of the advances in credit scoring from Fair, Issac and now others over the last 30 years, the empirically derived systems are by definition based on statistical analysis that is designed for the center of the bell curve. The computer misses a lot of deals at the tail of the bell curve that will pay like an A credit — but at 18% interest.

These factors create a compelling case for examining the subprime sector. However, before you make the final decision to jump into this market, even at this low point in the cycle, let's look at the cons.

RISKS OF SUBPRIME LOANS

The market reality of subprime loans is unfortunately much different than the theoretical benefits. One way of coming to terms with these market risks is to compare monthly and cumulative default rates of actual investor portfolios with models based on various assumptions about initial percentage of default. These comparisons appear on the following pages in exhibits 1 through 10.

In Exhibit 1, the default curve demonstrates the spike in defaults in the first nine months of a portfolio's life. The defaults become very low after month 32 due to the equity position of the collateral.

The portfolio demonstrated in Exhibit 2 was originated in Arizona. The climate, with the lack of ice and salt, may have helped preserve the collateral. The stronger collateral condition may account for the dramatic flattening of the cumulative default curve beginning in month 28.

Exhibit 1: Monthly Default % — Model versus Portfolio
Model Assumes a Default of 23%

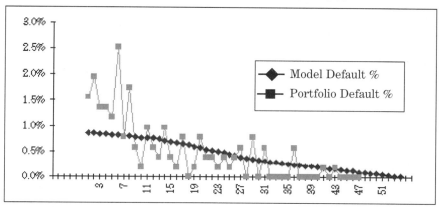

Exhibit 2: Cumulative Default % — Model versus Portfolio
Model Assumes a Default of 23%

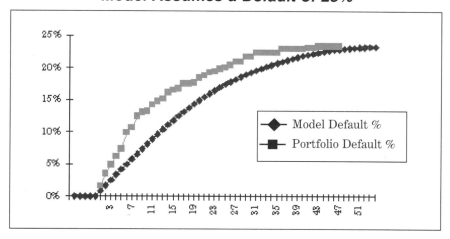

The spike in defaults in the first nine months, as shown in Exhibit 1, is also very likely to predict the spike when lifetime defaults are increased. The portfolio in Exhibit 3 performed at the projected lifetime default.

The cumulative curve in Exhibit 4 shows how defaults can come back to forecast at month 28, even after drifting outside the curve at month 10. The drift outside the cumulative default curve resulted primarily from the customer's lack of an equity in the collateral.

Exhibit 3: Monthly Default % — Model versus Portfolio
Model Assumes a Default of 30.96%

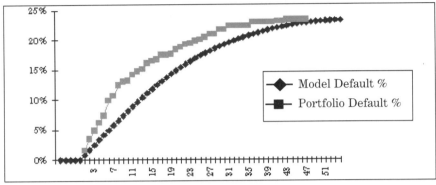

Exhibit 4: Cumulative Default % — Model versus Portfolio
Model Assumes a Default of 30.96%

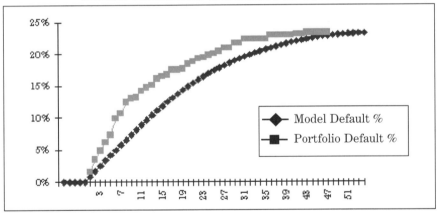

The monthly default percent noted in Exhibit 5 is from a portfolio of approximately 500 accounts. It demonstrates the extreme volatility of smaller pools.

The portfolio underlying Exhibit 6 looked as though it would break under the curve at month 18 — only to drift back out. It eventually came under the cumulative curve before it fully liquidated.

The portfolio in Exhibit 7 was purchased with buybacks from the seller on loans that defaulted during the first 90 days. It is also a small pool that shows a great deal of volatility.

Exhibit 5: Monthly Default % — Model versus Portfolio
Model Assumes a Default of 35%

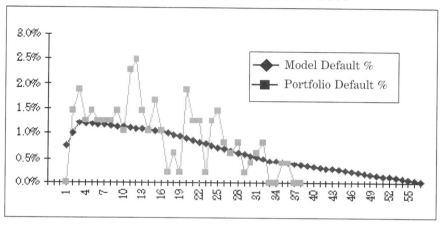

Exhibit 6: Cumulative Default % — Model versus Portfolio
Model Assumes a Default of 35%

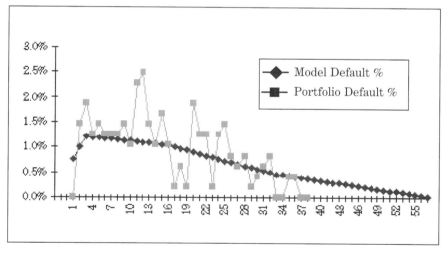

Even with zero defaults for the first 90 days, the portfolio in Exhibit 8 drifted outside the cumulative curve at month 12. The portfolio never recovered; it liquidated with defaults in excess of projections, thus demonstrating how difficult it can be to forecast defaults in excess of 35%.

The double spike in defaults of the pool in Exhibit 9 is common.

Exhibit 7: Monthly Default % — Model versus Portfolio
Model Assumes a Default of 40%

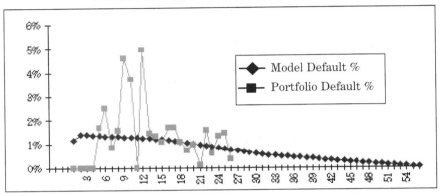

Exhibit 8: Cumulative Default % — Model versus Portfolio
Model Assumes a Default of 40%

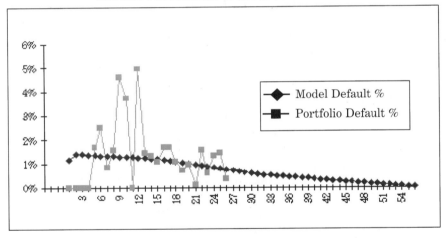

The first wave of defaults is incurred and collection efforts ramp up to correct the problem, only to see loans extended in month 7 default in month 11.

The portfolio in Exhibit 10 crossed the projected cumulative curve at month 8 and eventually recovered by the time it liquidated. It was able to recover mainly due to its relatively low loan-to-value at time of origination.

Exhibit 9: Monthly Default % — Model versus Portfolio
Model Assumes a Default of 45%

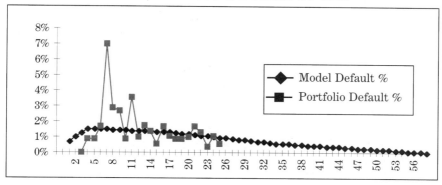

Exhibit 10: Cumulative Default % — Model versus Portfolio
Model Assumes a Default of 45%

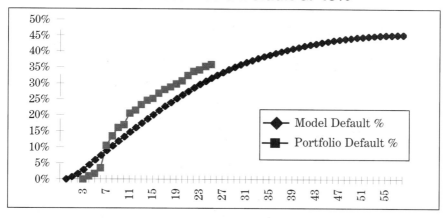

SOME POINTERS ON SUBPRIME RISK

Get to know the product you'll be dealing with by looking at it closely according to several key criteria.

- It is difficult to underwrite subprime paper that will pay consistently in volume levels above $1 million to $2 million per month. By the way, if an originator tells you he has B product, 90% of the time it's C. If you are told it's C, then you can almost bet the ranch it is D or worse. It takes a lot of declined A applications to gain decent volume. Since you may have an 80% decline rate even on the marginal pool and a funding rate that could only be about

70% of the initial 20% approved, it takes a lot of work to add much volume.

- Buying A credits is not direct experience for buying subprime. Because you must usually use a judgmental credit methodology, you may have difficulties (in maintaining volume and/or adhering to underwriting guidelines) if you add or change credit buyers.

- If you decide to buy a product from an existing originator, look past the underwriting guidelines to the actual loans. All of these shops have reasonable underwriting criteria. However, the implementation is where they often fall short. Remember, P.A.C. Brookline, Continental, Translending from the 1980s and the long list of recently failed companies that reportedly left banks and credit guarantee insurance companies with a number of bad loans that did not meet the established guidelines.

- The indirect auto business is noted for potential abuse and fraud. It doesn't happen that often but, when it does, it is as subtle as a sonic boom. In the arena of subprime credits, you can magnify the frequency of fraud and the "boom" by tenfold (Mercury comes to mind).

- If you get into a sinking ship, you usually don't find out until it is relatively late to minimize losses. The time it takes for one of these programs to come unwound is usually 24 to 36 months — longer if volume continues to increase year after year — thus creating the treadmill effect. By the time you identify problems, it's usually too late.

- Determine before you buy your first deal how the originator is compensated. If the originator's income is tied to its specific portfolio's performance, you are much better off than if the originator is paid for pure volume. For example, if the originator hits the dealer for five points up front (often called a "chop") and charges you two to three points on the backside regardless of the default rate, the temptation to approve loans can be overwhelming. Find a way to hold the originator accountable for the loan's performance. Part of what fueled the S&L crisis of the '80s was the manner in which land developers were paid up-front fees when the financing of a project was approved, without consideration of the project's viability or performance.

Chapter 7: Subprime Auto Paper: Promised Land or Nightmare?

Finally, if the originator participates in the profit from the sale of "aftermarket products" such as credit life or extended warranties, you should concern yourself with their basic business charter. Is the originator's core business only "sales" or "risk management" as it should be?

- Look behind the originator to the servicer on servicing-retained transactions. The world is full of "wannabe" originators that you can take a chance on if the principals are honest. A good servicer can make subprime credit pay almost like A credits but, unfortunately, the reverse is almost a certainty.

- Obviously, capitalization is an issue with an originator. But, with a servicer it is extremely important. Consider what happens to the delinquency on a group of subprime auto loans while you are lobbying a bankruptcy judge for six months for your credit files or even just a magnetic tape for conversion. The bottom line to this business is that the credit guys in this type of operation have to be able to weed through 10 declined loans to find two or three that will pay. Don't get confused by default insurance policies or reserve accounts. Those are only for the few that the credit guys are allowed to miss. Inside a subprime paper shop, reserves and default insurance policies are looked at almost as marketing expenses.

BUYING FROM AN EXISTING ORIGINATOR

If you have an interest in buying this type of asset from an existing originator, here are a few guidelines.

- Dust off and reread the Standard & Poor's structured finance February 1995 credit comment on "Securitization of Sub-Prime Automobile Loans" before you get too excited about this product. The October 25, 1995, "Financial Companies & Securitization" writeup by Equity Research of America is another good read. Finally, Moody's Special Report dated December 6, 1996, is also worth your time. It is a shame that so much quality work was published so long ago and we still have had so much fallout since then.
- If possible, deal only with a servicer that is rated Aa or higher by Moody's or the equivalent. (Are there any?)

- Avoid firms that have a huge and ever-expanding investor list that lends to the appearance that they can't get repeat business. This trend is especially troublesome if they keep moving farther from their physical location and/or original trade area.

- Perform professional background checks on the principles. Some of today's most renowned promoters were involved only a few years back with the firms that caused serious losses and, at times, lengthy litigation for bankers. Some of these promoters are even convicted felons.

- Watch out for firms with too many "chiefs" and not enough "Indians." This product attracts senior- to executive-vice-president types that often lack the technical skills needed in the trenches. You need to be able to hang your hat on an indirect automobile underwriter with at least 10 years of experience with entities such as banks, Ford Motor Credit Co. (FMCC), or General Motors Acceptance Corp. (GMAC).

- Risk-based equity is here to stay. Be careful with the leverage you use. If you are using 11.5 to 1 or higher, it may be better to lower it 7.5 to 1 or even 4 to 1.

- Buy seasoned product if you can and obtain performance data of the full original cohort of loans. It is simple but true: It's much easier to analyze the past than to predict the future.

- Be careful with your monthly liquidation assumptions. We should have learned this from the First Mortgage guys, but I guess we did not. You may experience 2.5% to 3.0% monthly liquidations early in the life of the portfolio.

- Think of Alan Greenspan's comments, before the financial market turmoil of 1998 but after the implosion of the subprime auto asset class, when he reflected that the economy was the best he had seen in 50 years. How will subprime auto portfolios perform during the next recession?

- Face the reality that this is asset-backed lending in its purest form. The value of the vehicle is central to the viability of the loans — as is the case with "location" for real estate; since the rate of default will always be relatively high. You need only remember three things: Equity! Equity!! Equity!!! The biggest trouble spot here is confusing down-payment with equity. If you can get 25% down and are still at 125% of the manufacturer's suggested retail price (MSRP), what have you gained? Answer: a large guaranteed loss when you call the repo man.

CONCLUSION

Before deciding whether this asset class is a promised land or a nightmare, review the results in the exhibits that appear earlier in this chapter and judge for yourself. My guess is somewhere in between.

Leonard Blum is a managing director of Westwood Capital, LLC. Blum has more than 12 years of investment banking and capital markets experience. Most recently, he was a managing director in the investment banking group of Prudential Securities Inc. During his 12-year tenure at Prudential, Blum served in a variety of capacities and was involved in many facets of investment banking and capital raising for companies in a variety of industries. He was a founding member of the asset-backed securities group and was later elevated to group head of that area.

Under Blum's guidance, Prudential achieved a No. 3 market share in ABS, was the No. 1 firm in home equity securities for six consecutive years, and dominated the issuance of securities backed by unguaranteed portions of SBA 7(a) loans.

As a pioneer in the ABS field, Blum has been involved in many cutting-edge transactions including the securitization of receivables backed by airline tickets, excess servicing, SBA loans, intellectual property, auto leases, equipment leases, auto loans, home equity loans, high LTV loans, alt-A mortgages, jumbo mortgages, agency mortgages, healthcare claims, private-label cards, credit cards, commercial mortgages, manufactured housing, and trade receivables.

Blum also has been involved with merger-and-acquisition work, initial and subsequent public offerings of common stock, subordinated debt, preferred stock, senior unsecured debt, and bankruptcy advisory work regarding receivables valuation and financing alternatives.

Blum holds bachelor's and master's degrees from California State University, as well as an MBA from UCLA Graduate School of Management as a Carter Fellow. A frequent lecturer, Blum has spoken at or chaired a great number of industry conferences. His writings on ABS have been published, including numerous chapters in two books edited by Frank J. Fabozzi.

Chapter 8

Home Equity Loans*

Leonard Blum
Managing Director
Westwood Capital, LLC

A home-equity mortgage loan allows a homeowner to tap his or her embedded home equity, in return for which the originator is granted a lien on that borrower's residence. Home-equity loans can be either lines of credit (HELOCs) or closed-end (HELs). Within these broad groupings, loans have a wide variety of credit, prepayment, contractual characteristics, and lien positions (first, second, or other.)

This chapter reviews the various features of home-equity loans and explores the dynamics of what has been one of the fastest-growing areas of the HEL market: the nonprime credit (B&C) sector.

LOAN CHARACTERISTICS

Use of Proceeds

The common uses of HEL proceeds are home improvement, education, debt consolidation, medical expense, business needs, and other major purchases. The use of proceeds can provide insight into the performance of a loan. For example, home improvement loans often have stronger credit characteristics because the use of proceeds increases the value of the collateral. These loans are also likely to prepay more slowly in the early years of origination as a borrower is much less likely to sell a home that was recently improved.

With respect to debt consolidation, repayment of existing debt may not be a borrower's initial goal. Instead, it may be suggested by the originator, especially in the case of B&C loans for which the originator may serve the dual function of credit counselor and lender. HELs usually are tax-deductible with lower rates than other forms of consumer cred-

---

*The author would like to acknowledge and thank Morton Dear and Henry C. McCall III for their help and guidance in the preparation of this chapter.

it (such as credit cards), allowing the consumer to economize on debt service charges. Additionally, if a borrower's aggregate payment can be decreased through consolidation, the probability of that borrower's default can be reduced. Note, however, that critics of debt consolidation argue that such refinancing activity can increase the consumer's ability to access additional credit. Once consumers have repaid debts, the potential to draw upon credit lines is increased, thereby potentially increasing aggregate debt service and the likelihood of default.

Increasingly, HELs are being used to consolidate and refinance existing mortgage debt. For obvious reasons, such consolidation and refinancing is likely to occur with greater frequency in a low-interest-rate environment Also, increased industry competition and the presence of loan brokers in the origination channel have caused targeted refinancings, where borrowers with existing HELs are offered lower payments or larger, consolidated loans. Nonetheless, mortgage debt consolidation not only increases loan sizes but also potentially benefits consumers by consolidating debt at lower interest rates. From a lender's perspective, potential loss severity is reduced as the consolidated first-lien position is not subordinated to other lenders. Moreover, mortgage consolidation and refinancing loans are larger, which increases the originator's income from interest, points, and servicing. Historically, the HEL market was known as the "second mortgage industry." Because existing mortgage debt is now generally consolidated, this "second mortgage" designation is no longer appropriate.

Open- and Closed-End Loans

A HELOC grants the homeowner a line of credit against the embedded equity in his or her home. The consumer generally draws part of the balance at closing and makes additional draws by writing checks during a "revolving" period of 10 to 15 years, following which there is either an amortization period or a balloon payment. Some HELOCs do not have revolving periods; instead, each drawn balance is amortized over a set period. Additional draws adjust the monthly payment in an amount sufficient to amortize the then-outstanding balance over the loan's term.

HELs are closed-end loans, which can have fixed or floating rates of interest. These mortgages generally fully amortize over 10 to 30 years, although some have balloon payments due in five, 10, or 15 years. HELs usually are level-payment loans for which the consumer makes a fixed payment each month. In the early years of a loan, a larger percentage of this payment is allocated to interest whereas, in the later years, a larger percentage is allocated to principal.

In contrast to mortgages that amortize on an actuarial basis (as is the case with agency-conforming mortgages), HELs usually are simple-interest loans. With an actuarial loan, a borrower pays a precomputed amount of interest in a given month as long as the payment is received before a specified date. If the payment is received after that date, the lender assesses a late charge. Conversely, in a simple-interest loan, the amount of interest due each month varies based on the number of days elapsed since the lender last received a payment.

Adjustable-rate HELs (ARMs) bear interest relative to an index, which is often the London interbank offered rate (LIBOR). Generally, LIBOR ARMs are teasered. A teasered loan has an initial rate of interest that is lower than its margin plus its index. These loans also have life and periodic caps. Life caps limit the maximum interest rate a borrower will pay in any given period during the life of the loan (life caps often are set at 6% over the teaser). Periodic caps limit the maximum amount the rate can change at each reset date. Some of these loans also have floors; in some cases the floor is set at or near the teaser.

MARKETS

Borrower Characteristics

B&C borrowers have blemished credit histories; however, lenders have been able to service this market segment profitably for several reasons. First, the security provided by a borrowe'rs home may justify a loan to a borrower to whom a lender may not otherwise be willing to extend credit. Since these loans often have low loan-to-value (LTV) ratios — and lenders focus carefully on LTV adequacy and appraisal accuracy — the risk inherent in lending to this group of borrowers is significantly reduced. Second, many originators carefully analyze borrower credit and use underwriting techniques that allow them to identify borrowers that have a high probability of satisfying a loan, as discussed later in this chapter. Also, the higher rates charged to these borrowers compensate lenders for the increased risk and the more intense origination, servicing, and collection procedures inherent with these loans.

Even within the B&C universe, there is a wide range of borrower credit quality. Some borrowers have steady sources of income and only modestly blemished credit. Others have weak credit but significant home equity to secure a loan. Some originators specialize in a given homeowner demographic/credit sector whereas others balance their underwriting guidelines and loan pricing to accommodate a wide diversity of borrower profiles.

Origination

B&C originators gather loans directly or indirectly. Direct origination occurs when a lender markets directly to a borrower or originates directly through correspondent brokers. Indirect origination occurs when a lender purchases loans, either one at a time or in pools from other lenders or brokers. Typical direct marketing channels include television, newspapers, radio, direct mail, and the Internet. Larger originators enjoy significant advertising economies of scale and often can exploit mixed media campaigns, causing such entities to build market share at rapid rates.

Some lenders purchase third-party loans to supplement their existing business. Others originate exclusively through indirect channels. Experienced originators perform careful due diligence to ascertain the quality of third-party originations; they examine not only the seller's business practices but also the homeowner's credit and the quality of collateral. When properly administered, an indirect lending operation can be a strong supplement to an originator's retail flow or a logical business strategy.

Underwriting

B&C home-equity lending is sometimes misunderstood by those familiar with traditional mortgage origination. Prime mortgage originators underwrite with strict, formulaic methods. These methods use minimum borrower requirements, such as strong credit records and low debt-to-income ratios. Although HEL origination does utilize some formulas and credit scoring, this type of lending is more flexible; credit-impaired borrowers often have complex credit profiles. Competent HEL underwriters understand how to "look through the numbers" and assess a borrower's ability to repay. Still, in underwriting loans to credit-impaired borrowers, controlled delinquency levels should be expected. Even with such delinquency levels, net losses generally are low and have hovered below 1 % for the industry.

B&C borrowers have credit blemishes that range from minor delinquencies to bankruptcies. Also, their debt-to-income ratios may be high. Some borrowers may be strong credits, yet they may have suffered a temporary setback. For example, they may have been displaced in an economic contraction and may have found reemployment at a lower salary level. As discussed, to mitigate the risks of lending to B&C borrowers, lenders require LTV ratios that are significantly lower than those found with loans made to conforming borrowers. For example, many home-equity originators shun making loans with LTVs of 80% or more, whereas 80% LTVs are commonplace in the conforming market.

While the average LTV for a "typical" B&C pool may be 65% to 70%, conforming loan pools can average 70% to 75%. B&C lenders generally charge more points and/or higher yields, which significantly compensate for the additional cash-flow risk. These mitigating factors have allowed finance companies to fulfill an important social function by providing credit to a vastly underserved market: Only a minority of the American public has unblemished credit histories.

When underwriting a loan, an originator generally focuses on both the ability of a borrower to repay and the adequacy of that borrower's collateral. Although most originators prefer to have both factors present, some will focus more on one factor than the other. For example, some lenders originate loans with very low LTV ratios and may focus less on a borrower's credit history or the ratio of a borrower's gross debt service to income. Still, they still will not make a loan if their subjective evaluation suggests that a borrower may be unable to repay and foreclosure would be expected.

Other lenders focus primarily on borrower credit and may make loans with LTV ratios in excess of 70% or even 80%, but only will extend such loans to their most creditworthy borrowers. These low LTVs account for low expected loss severities in the event of default (and mitigated foreclosure frequency). Low LTVs also can mitigate the lack of transactional verification of value. With purchase-money mortgages, the "value" component (the denominator) of LTV is the lesser of the purchase price or the appraised value.

When assessing credit quality, originators often view mortgage delinquencies differently than delinquencies to credit card or automobile loans. Originators generally will tolerate high levels of historical non-mortgage delinquencies (relative to their tolerance levels for mortgage delinquencies). Originators will study a borrower's credit over specific time periods (e.g., one or two years). They will require that, for a specific grade of loan, a borrower's frequency and severity of delinquency on specific debt has not exceeded certain limitations. Originators also review a borrower's previous judgements, foreclosures, and bankruptcies. Other considerations include level of documentation (full versus limited documentation), property types (e.g., high-rise versus low-rise condominiums or single-family, detached homes), and occupancy status (e.g., second homes and investor properties versus primary residences).

Grading

Originators commonly grade their loans. They use designations such as A, B, C, or D (sometimes with pluses and minuses within grades). One confusing feature, however, is the lack of grading standardization among originators. One originator's A– could be another lender's B. Hopefully, the criteria used by the rating agencies, the sureties, and the large originators will standardize this diversity over time. As a lender moves from A to D, maximum allowable LTVs decline while debt-to-income ratios increase and allowable credit histories deteriorate. Many originators will further limit LTVs if alternate verifications of income are used or the property type is perceived as risky. Regardless of the originator's philosophy, it is important for an originator to be consistent in limiting LTV as other perceived risks increase.

Due to the reliance on LTVs, appraisal procedures and quality control programs are important. Obviously, an LTV is meaningful only if the appraisal is accurate. Although many originators use outside appraisers, such originators generally have strict review policies and strict approval processes for new appraisers. Originators carefully monitor appraisers through reviews and reappraisals. Appraisers with significant adjustments are removed from approved status. Low LTV ratios and strong appraisal controls are the cornerstone of several home-equity programs. Credit underwriting decisions also are often carefully re-underwritten. Experience by broker is often tracked. Originators also monitor performance by in-house personnel. Re-review of delinquent and defaulted loans is commonplace to determine if errors were made or policies should be altered.

Servicing

B&C borrowers are more likely to become delinquent than A borrowers. Notably, these borrowers are far more sensitive than their conforming quality counterparts to the quality and intensity of servicing. Generally, the lower grade the borrower, the more intense the servicing procedures should be; therefore, servicers contact delinquent B&C homeowners early and often. These servicers maintain intense contact throughout a delinquency cycle. As a delinquency progresses, the frequency and intensity of calls increases. Lenders realize that many borrowers, due to high debt loads and lack of financial resources, will find it difficult to recover if they miss a payment.

INDUSTRY HISTORY

Early Lending Dynamics

In the 1960s, B&C home-equity lending was virtually nonexistent. Nonprime borrowers generally received loans only for a specific purpose, such as the purchase of a consumer durable. Over time, finance companies — historically the lenders to the nonprime market — realized that such consumers had additional borrowing needs. Due to some degree of blemished credit histories, nonprime consumers had limited funding resources. However, these consumers did own homes, which could serve as collateral for loans. Lenders also recognized from experience that these consumers were generally creditworthy, even if they were occasionally delinquent. In the 1970s, finance companies began to originate B&C HELs. Some of the early finance companies included institutions such as Aames, United Companies Financial Corporation, The Money Store, and Advanta.

In its early stages, the industry was extremely fragmented due to a lack of capital. Often, lenders funded themselves with retained earnings and loan sales. Non-warehouse, direct institutional equity and debt were generally unavailable to such lenders. As a result, their ability to make loans was limited. A typical origination strategy involved gradually building a loan portfolio and using the cash flow from this portfolio to make additional loans. Over time, borrowers had additional financing needs and could be refinanced. In many ways, in this environment, a company's portfolio represented the franchise value of its business. Often, the customer base was built through referrals from friends and family.

Finance companies could access warehouse lines on a limited basis. There were a few banks extending credit to finance companies in the 1970s and 1980s; however, the outstanding lines generally were small. The warehouse lines that did exist had high interest rates (prime rate plus 100 basis points or more) and low advance rates (usually 80% to 85% of principal balance but sometimes as high as 90%), which stretched precious capital. Capital was tight even for the better finance companies, and daily cash management was an art. Yet because these lines had recourse and low advance rates, lenders could originate and warehouse loans with a wide variety of characteristics. For example, lenders made church and multipurpose loans, broadly serving their communities.

Finance companies also sold whole loans on both recourse and nonrecourse bases as a financing source. Sometimes, the recourse was limited. For example, it could be restricted in the aggregate to one investor or a specific loan pool. Early investors included banks and wealthy individuals, and many loans were sold servicing-retained (i.e., the seller of a loan continued to service such loan for an ongoing fee). In the mid 1980s, the whole-loan market broadened, and finance companies increased their sales of loans to banks, insurance companies and savings and loan associations.

Turning Points

During the late 1980s, the HEL industry enjoyed several watershed events. The Tax Reform Act of 1986 (the Act) created an impetus for the growth of the primary and securitized markets. First, the Act created the Real Estate Mortgage Investment Conduit (REMIC) rules, which allowed the tax-efficient structuring of multiclass HEL securitizations. Second, tax legislation phased out the deductibility of most nonmortgage consumer debt. Since interest on HELs generally is deductible, this form of debt became relatively more attractive to the consumer At the same time, participants in the market realized the potential of asset securitization as a way to fund growth. As a result, originators started securitizing HELs. These early securitizations were small, private placements, structured as a single-class and surety-wrapped. These transactions, which occurred in the late 1980s, paved the way for home-equity originators to gain direct access to the institutional capital markets.

Securitization allowed originators to grow dramatically. This growth attracted equity capital which, in turn, funded the negative cash flow characteristics of securitization (discussed later in this chapter). By the mid 1990s, equity capital was readily available to HEL originators, which further fueled growth, thereby leading to ever-increasing securitization volumes.

Consumers were the beneficiary of the industry's increased access to capital, as home equity loans became widely available to this previously underserved market Competition increased as existing lenders gained capital access and new originators emerged. Finance companies could now finance their production at a low cost through securitization, without excessive reliance on piecemeal sales at relatively high implied funding costs. Consumers increasingly were able to refinance outstanding debts at lower interest rates, reduce their monthly payments (due to both lower rates and longer maturities of the HEL vis-a-vis other consumer debt), enjoy the tax advantages of mortgage borrowing, and fund major expenditures.

Initially, finance companies were the dominant nonprime lenders; more recently (generally beginning in 1997), depositories have become active B&C HEL originators. Banks, however, as a general matter, still prefer to serve the upper credit tier of this market.

Capital is King

During 1998, the financial markets became less receptive to finance company HEL originators. Equity prices fell as numerous originators wrote down their excess servicing assets. Rating and equity analysts downgraded issuers. The subordinated debt and equity markets, which traditionally had been used by finance companies to fund the negative cash flow characteristics of securitization, became unavailable. As issuers increasingly turned to the whole-loan market as a quasi-capital source, a supply/demand imbalance was created, and whole loan prices fell dramatically. Warehouse providers, in reaction to these factors, pulled credit lines, which exacerbated the situation. Additionally, asset-backed spreads widened dramatically — generally doubling — in the second half of the year due to a global fixed-income "flight to quality" and massive bond sales by hedge funds and Wall Street firms.

These capital factors had a dramatic effect on the industry. Several large finance companies filed for bankruptcy protection. Others were acquired or found capital partners. Mergers and acquisitions for 1998 are detailed in Exhibit 1. Still others remained independent and continued to prosper, either via capital access through a well capitalized parent (for example, RFC, which is indirectly owned by General Motors) or specific forms of sustainable, competitive advantage in both financing and operating activities, such as American Business Credit. Access to capital has become the single most important source of competitive advantage.

Exhibit 1: Selected M&A Activity During 1998

	Acquirer/Partner	*Target/Partner*
Dec.	BNC Mortgage, Inc.	America's Lender, Inc.
Dec.	Green Point Financial Corp.	Headlands Mortgage Co.
Dec.	Westmark Group Holdings Inc.	Credit Depot Corp.
Nov.	Greenwich Street Capital	IMC Mortgage Co.
Oct.	U.S. Bancorp	New Century Financial Corp.
Sept.	Fremont General Corp.	Pacific America
June	Conseco Inc.	Green Tree Financial Corp.
April	Household International, Inc.	Beneficial Corp.
Feb.	First Union Corp.	The Money Store, Inc.

Source: Westwood Capital, LLC Database

Exacerbation of Stratification

The market has always been stratified into whole-loan sellers, on the one hand, and portfolio lenders/securitizers on the other. Whole-loan sellers generally are small, nondepository enterprises without significant access to capital. Securitizers and portfolio lenders generally possess greater access to capital, are either depositories or well capitalized nondepositories, and gather loans through direct and indirect originations. Traditionally, a large number of small brokers have sold whole loans to portfolio lenders and/or securitizers. The Liquidity Crisis of 1998 intensified the distinction between whole-loan sellers and securitizers/lenders.

BENEFITS OF ASSET SECURITIZATION

Because of securitization's major role in the industry's growth, no discussion about the industry would be complete without a discussion of this financing tool. As the HEL securitization market has grown, it has allowed originators to accomplish several strategic objectives.

Improved Asset/Liability Management

Asset securitization allows an originator to "match fund" assets and liabilities. This benefit is particularly important with fixed-rate HELs. By selling fixed-rate "liabilities" that are effectively callable as mortgages prepay, an originator has partially — but not completely — transferred interest rate risk. Nonetheless, some degree of risk remains on an issuer's balance sheet in the form of capitalized excess servicing. If rates fall, a modest pickup in prepayments should occur, which would reduce the value of the retained asset. Note, however, that B&C borrowers have demonstrated significantly less sensitivity than prime-quality borrowers to changes in interest rates; prepayments on these loans have remained relatively stable through interest rate swings.

In the case of LIBOR ARMs funded with floating-rate ABS, the cash flows on the underlying asset are defined by periodic and lifetime caps, whereas the securities pay interest based on a floating index and are limited to "available funds" (after covering certain trust expenses). Because an originator's excess servicing (ongoing interest in the trust) is represented by the difference between payments on the assets and the securities, this cash flow could deteriorate in certain rate scenarios. This risk can be transferred to investors if the securities are structured as pass-throughs. Yet, this generally raises an originator's funding costs; obviously, investors demand a higher return for taking on this incremental risk.

Improved Velocity of Capital

Securitization has allowed finance company originators to increase the velocity of their capital. By selling loans and using the capital markets to transfer interest rate and funding risks, the finance company can focus its capital on the areas of the business that it knows best: marketing, originating, and servicing loans — not funding them.

Improved Credit Discipline
The securitization market has imposed credit discipline. Portfolios are scrutinized by investment bankers, investors, sureties, and rating agencies prior to securitization. Riskier portfolios are measurably more expensive to securitize; this fact forces originators to understand the real cost of a given loan's attributes. They must decide whether to charge the homeowner a different rate, restructure the loan, or not make the loan.

Control of Leverage
Under generally accepted accounting principles (GAAP), securitization is treated as a sale of assets. This allows an originator to grow market share without increasing accounting leverage (or bumping up against loan covenants).

Acceleration of Earnings
Securitization enhances an originator's revenue stream. When an originator securitizes, it recognizes a gain on sale based on the present value of its retained interest in the securitization plus its net proceeds. This benefit also brings a drawback: It potentially increases the volatility of earnings.

SECURITIZATION VERSUS WHOLE-LOAN SALES
When an originator securitizes loans, it sells an at or near "par coupon" security and retains "excess servicing" — the difference between the interest component of the loans and the ongoing securitization expenses, including the interest rate paid to investors. The sum of the net cash proceeds from the securitization and the noncash present value of the retained excess servicing generally is greater than the cash proceeds an originator would receive from a servicing-retained sale of the loans.

- An originator will have a higher present value if it securitizes than if it had sold whole loans. This generally is because its retained excess servicing is greater than the premium it would have received in a whole-loan sale.

- Compared with a whole-loan sale, the cash proceeds at closing are lower in a securitization. This is an important consideration for many smaller, "cash-strapped" originators, who may not have sufficient access to capital to fund their excess servicing.

- When an originator securitizes loans, it receives cash flow equal to the net proceeds at closing. Yet it must pay origination costs and taxes on its gain on sale. Some of this cash outlay is financed by the points it charges borrowers. Still, for many originators, securitization, although superior from a present-value perspective, can cause negative cash flow, especially in a fast-growth scenario.

- Compared with a whole-loan sale, an originator generally retains more risk in a securitization. This is because an originator often retains prepayment and credit risk in the form of its excess servicing asset.

- A hybrid form of sale/securitization is to securitize and then sell some of the excess servicing. This can be achieved, by way of example, by securitizing an originator's excess servicing asset. Depending on the specifics of such a transaction, the economic outcome will be between a whole loan sale and a securitization.

STANDARDIZATION OF THE MARKET

Securitization has increased the standardization of B&C home equity loans. Prior to the advent of securitization, lenders made loans in their community secured by a variety of collateral types. Church loans, mixed-use multifamily loans, and other real estate loans were not uncommon. The advent of securitization also led to a higher degree of homogeneity in loan pools for a variety of reasons, although other collateral types are still sometimes securitized as a separate tranche of a HEL transaction. Sureties and rating agencies either required high levels of subordination for nonhomogeneous or high-risk pools or rejected them outright. Investors prefer homogenous pools. As many lenders originate for sale into the secondary market, they have either discontinued originating loans that are unacceptable for securitization or costly to securitize, retained their nonsecuritizable originations in portfolio and charged a higher rate on these loans than otherwise would be the case, or sold these loans in whole-loan form while securitizing their other originations.

INVESTOR CONSIDERATIONS

In view of these considerations, investors should increasingly incorporate the following in their evaluation of securitized HELs in addition to the relative-value analysis of the securities:

- How well is the originator capitalized?

- How long has the originator been in business?
- Is the management team stable and experienced in consumer (not conforming mortgage) credit?
- Is the originator investing side by side with the investor? Has the originator retained or sold the excess servicing in the transaction?
- Does the originator have a lending philosophy? Do they stick to that philosophy, even at the cost of slower growth?
- What is the originator's servicing experience?

SUMMARY

The majority of American borrowers have some credit blemish. Lenders increasingly are providing loans to credit-impaired borrowers. As a result, they are providing credit to a previously underserved market and performing a valuable social function. Although loan terms generally compensate lenders for the additional credit risk in this sector, lenders have developed policies and procedures to control risk.

Securitization initially allowed the HEL industry to grow dramatically. It also has standardized HEL lending and imposed a higher degree of credit discipline. During 1998, institutions with deep access to capital gained significant competitive advantages. Those that lacked capital resources increasingly filled a broker role, selling their production on a whole-loan basis to well-heeled institutions. Despite the dramatic changes in the industry's competitive landscape, HEL lending continues to grow. Because of the benefits to both borrower and lender alike, we expect continued growth in this sector, albeit at a slower rate.

Frank L. Raiter is a managing director in structured finance ratings at Standard & Poor's. Raiter joined S&P in 1995 from Caliber Bank, Phoenix, where he served as treasurer and chief investment officer.

Earlier in his career, Raiter was assistant director with the securities transaction group at Resolution Trust Corporation. He has extensive knowledge of mortgage-backed securities and derivatives from the investment management and issuer/sales perspectives.

Raiter is a graduate of North Carolina State University and holds a master's degree in business administration from the University of North Carolina.

Chapter 9

Risk-Based Pricing Nonagency Mortgages And Securities

Frank L. Raiter
Managing Director, Structured Finance Ratings
Standard & Poor's

The evolution of mortgage underwriting technology and risk analyses that has occurred since mid-1995 has created a number of unique opportunities for mortgage bankers, issuers, and investors. One of the most enticing opportunities that has arisen from this technology is the ability of mortgage originators and portfolio managers to apply risk-based pricing techniques to individual loans. The developments in these techniques are a direct result of the implementation of automated underwriting systems that incorporate statistical mortgage scoring capabilities. These scoring systems have driven the refinements to analytical models that provide the information necessary for investors to gauge the relative risk of an individual loan and to establish a price or, conversely, a coupon reflecting the inherent risk.

AUTOMATED UNDERWRITING SYSTEMS

The automated underwriting systems that are currently available include GE Capital Mortgage Insurance Co.'s Omni System, MGIC's LPS, PMI's Aura, and UGI's AccuScore. These systems share the same fundamental advantages of objectivity, consistency, speed, and efficiency. In addition, each of these systems incorporates to some extent advances in technology that provide for the verification of key elements of the application such as income and employment. Several of these systems also incorporate links that provide access to advanced systems for alternative collateral assessment, mortgage insurance evaluation, and other subsystem routines that further streamline the single-family mortgage application process.

    These improvements in systems design and data accumulation will all reduce the time associated with processing a mortgage application and, therefore, reduce the associated costs. However, it is the advances in statistical mortgage scoring that have been the engine that has driven the market so rapidly toward the potential of risk-based pricing and integrating risk management.

MORTGAGE SCORING

A mortgage score, by common definition, is a calculated numeric score that represents the probability of a mortgage default. Mortgage scores have a significant advantage over manual underwriting. This advantage is a result of the number and diversity of variables that a scoring model can manipulate in arriving at a conclusion versus a human underwriter poring through a thick paper file.

Most mortgage scoring systems address the key aspects of the mortgage file, including application data such as employment, residence, and down payment information, and borrower capacity data, including assets, reserves, income, and overall borrower liabilities. In addition, mortgage scoring systems look at borrower credit data that include previous credit performance, timing, and usage of credit, and the various types of credit a borrower utilizes. Finally, scoring systems look at mortgage-specific data, including property type, financing type (first lien, second lien, or cashout/refinance), and the type of loan product (fixed-rate, adjustable, or other) that is represented by the proposed mortgage note. The scoring systems reviewed and calibrated by Standard & Poor's weighted the key variables according to their proprietary formulas, yet each provided a high degree of predictability.

The analyses and research that have been completed by the sponsors of the models and the analysts at Standard & Poor's substantiated the premise that mortgage scores are both objective and consistent. As a result of Standard & Poor's calibration process, a loan that is run through the mortgage scoring systems that have been validated and mapped by Standard & Poor's would receive the same risk grade regardless of the scoring system used. The same cannot always be said for a loan that is reviewed by five underwriters applying standard guidelines with subjective exception rules.

In addition, mortgage scoring systems have proved to be highly consistent. A loan that is scored on a particular system will receive the same score two weeks later, as long as no variables have been altered.

Mortgage scores also have proved to be highly predictive of the probability of the mortgage default or loss. Therefore, these scores allow better management of credit risk than bucketing by guidelines interpreted by underwriters at the time of origination.

SETTING A NEW STANDARD

While mortgage scores were one of the critical developments in the evolution of the mortgage market, the proliferation of scoring systems did not provide the industry with one easily applied standard for risk-ordering loans based on the new technology. As a result, Standard & Poor's, working with the major score system sponsors, mapped the scores of these systems into a matrix that allowed a consistent system of risk-grading loans to be established. These risk grades (RG1-RG7) reflect default probabilities based on mortgage scores. Therefore, they contain the same elements of objectivity and consistency that are inherent in the underlying scoring systems.

The Standard & Poor's risk grades RG1-RG7 are intended to replace the current underwriting guideline base system of A, A–, B, C, and D, as shown in Exhibit 1. In particular, the objectivity and consistency of the mortgage scores in the jumbo and subprime arena provide, for the first time, a standard that can easily be applied to any new or existing loan.

Exhibit 1: Standard & Poor's Risk Grades

RG1	Superior-quality loans exhibiting the lowest potential of default.
RG2	Above-average quality, expected to outperform the market overall.
RG3	Average quality loans exhibit default rates generally expected of loans underwritten to guidelines.
RG4	Slightly below the quality exhibited by agency underwriting.
RG5	Loans exhibiting default expectations that are considerably higher than the average loan.
RG6	Loan with default rates at significant multiples of the average-quality loans.
RG7	Loan exhibiting the highest risk of default.

Regardless of the originating institution, given an adequate amount of data, including current credit information, a mortgage can be scored and assigned a Standard & Poor's risk grade reflecting the loan's current likelihood of default. While some scoring systems built into automated underwriting systems can only score a loan at origination, the algorithm incorporated in Standard & Poor's LEVELS™ model can score loans any time using a standard data tape with a current Fair Isaac Corp. (FICO) score.

RISK-BASED PRICING

The standardization of risk grades tied to default probabilities provides the link to the analytical models that integrate the mortgage characteristics and pricing in the secondary market. Standard & Poor's has developed its LEVELS™ model to analyze individual mortgage loans and assign the appropriate risk grade. The LEVELS™ model uses the standard mortgage data file to compute estimated loss coverage requirements for residential mortgage loans or pools of loans based on Standard & Poor's rating criteria. The model consists of the following six primary subroutines:

- Quality control.
- Risk grade assignment.
- Foreclosure frequency adjustments.
- Loss severity estimation.
- Loss estimates.
- Generation of credit-enhancement levels.

The quality-control module checks each record in a loan data file to identify missing and/or incorrectly defined fields. The model generates output reports that identify any problems detected and, if not corrected, the reports will identify the assumptions that the model uses in order to complete the analyses. Risk grades assigned are based on the scores from validated mortgage scoring systems. If there is no validated mortgage score, the LEVELS™ model will assign a risk grade based on its internal mortgage scoring algorithm. Loan files submitted to Standard & Poor's that include FICO scores will receive mortgage scores from the LEVELS™ model. These scores then will be mapped into the risk grades. The model adjusts the foreclosure rates associated with the mortgage score based on the prime pool characteristics.

The next major calculations performed by the LEVELS™ model relate to the estimation of the expected loss severity associated with the given loan predicated on the assumed market value decline of the property in the event that foreclosure occurs. Estimates for liquidation expenses associated with foreclosure including brokerage fees, legal fees, taxes, and accrued interest payable are incorporated in these estimates. Loss severity estimates are developed as a percentage of the original loan values and converted to an estimated dollar amount. The loss estimates are then used as a basis for developing loss coverage or credit enhancement levels necessary to protect investors under different economic scenarios for different classes of rated securities. The ratings range from AAA to B. LEVELS™ then provides output for investors or for issuers pooling mortgages for securities. The output comprises the following three main elements:

- Risk grade of the associated loan.
- Loss estimate of the loan.
- Range of credit enhancement requirements associated with the particular loan or pool of loans

The information provided by the LEVELS™ analytics lends itself to several key risk-management activities of portfolio managers, investors, and secondary market professionals. These include risk grading, which stratifies a portfolio across seven risk grades that are currently available. The information also allows gauging loan-loss reserve requirements based on the loss estimates on a loan-by-loan and portfolio basis. Last but not least, the opportunities for risk-based pricing and its subsets of decision management include establishing risk-adjusted coupons at the time loans are originated and best-execution analysis at origination between whole-loan sale or securitization. Tools for the portfolio manager include marking portfolios to market, stratifying portfolios for liquidity, and performing best-execution analyses of the whole-loan and securitization options. Finally, the information provided can benefit in servicing management, as the intensity of servicing required is a function of a loan risk grade. In addition, by periodically calculating FICO scores on a portfolio of current mortgages, the complexion of the risk of a portfolio can be updated and the full range of value calculations completed for asset/liability management and interest rate risk measurement.

A SIMPLIFIED APPROACH TO RISK-BASED PRICING

Risk-based pricing can now be implemented at the point of origination because of the advances made in loan risk grade standardization coupled with the availability of credit enhancement requirements on a loan-by-loan basis, as shown in Exhibit 2. The credit enhancement requirements can then be used to map an individual loan transaction into the secondary market's pricing mechanism.

This mapping can take place through structuring a synthetic transaction, as market prices are only available through specific rated bonds that have been recently sold to investors (see Exhibit 3). In the prime loan arena the predominant structure is the senior/subordinated passthrough. In the subprime arena the predominant structure uses the excess spread-bond insured structure, although issuers are interested in extending the senior/subordinated passthrough structure to the subprime market.

Exhibit 2: LEVELS™ Output

Prime Loan		Credit Enhancement Requirement (%)	
Risk grade = RG1			
Collateral information			
Balance ($)	100,000	AAA	6.00
WAC (%)	8.0	AA	3.64
WAM (mos.)	360	A	2.55
WALA (mos.)	3	BBB	1.82
WALTV (%)	76.7	BB	0.91
Full doc. (%)	100	B	0.46
		N.R.	N.R

WALA = Weighted average loan age. N.R. = Not rated

Exhibit 3: Structuring a Synthetic Transaction

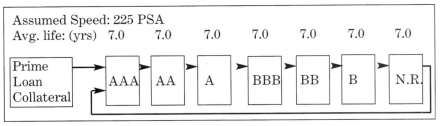

Using one of the readily available structuring systems, the sized classes can be structured and prepayment speeds applied to determine average lives for each bond and a coupon set. In the example shown in Exhibit 4, the coupon selected is 7.5%, creating an interest-only (IO) strip of 50 basis points to cover servicing and provide some excess to the originator.

In establishing a risk-based pricing mechanism, the value of a loan must be defined in its entirety so that the various pieces — including the net coupon, the servicing fees, up-front points, origination costs, securitization costs, and required rates of return on equit — must all be factored into the calculation. The market value of the risk associated with an individual loan or portfolio is established by the private-label MBS market by looking at the spreads to Treasuries for AAA through N.R. and IO strips of transactions that were recently brought to market. Establishing a synthetic securitization allows the real-time couponing of a loan against the current spreads in the market place.

Exhibit 4: Bond Size and Pricing

Rating	Size ($)	Coupon (%)	Price	Proceeds ($)
AAA	94,000,000	7.5	100.0	94,000,000
AA	2,360,000	7.5	99.4	2,345,840
A	1,090,000	7.5	97.0	1,057,300
BBB	730,000	7.5	94.6	690,580
BB	910,000	7.5	87.0	791,700
B	460,000	7.5	64.0	294,400
N.R.	460,000	7.5	30.0	135,000
Total	100,000,000			99,314,820

N.R. = Not rated

In Exhibit 4, the synthetic structure has been established and each bond priced against the current Treasury curve. The gross proceeds at $99,314,820 equate to a price of 99.3 versus funding at par. A review of the proceeds analysis takes into account the other economic variables integral to appropriately sizing the loan coupon and providing for best execution comparisons (see Exhibit 5). In this example, the proceeds are augmented by the value of the IO strip and reduced by the costs associated with servicing the loan, securitizing a transaction, and providing a return to the originator's capital. After making these adjustments, the loan has achieved a value of $99,610,000. The risk-based pricing adjustment to bring the loan to breakeven is an additional IO strip of 10 basis points. In other words, adding 10 basis points to the coupon (raising it to 8.10% from 8.00%) provides the originator with sufficient coupon to break even on securitization, retain the servicing, and enjoy a return on capital. From a best-execution perspective, should the whole-loan bid be in excess of 100, the originator adds to the return originating the loan.

Exhibit 5: Proceeds Analysis

Bonds proceeds		$99,314,820
IO (loan @ 8.00%)	50 bps @ $100,000,000	2,000,000
Minus		
	PV servicing	(510,000)
	Securitization fee 0.50	(500,000)
	ROE	(694,820)
		$99,610,000
Plus IO 10 basis points:		390,000
Adjusted loan coupon = 8.10%		$100,000,000

UNIQUE DIMENSION ADDED

Risk-based pricing can be applied to new volumes at the time applications are underwritten or adapted to risk-grading and valuing seasoned portfolios for asset/liability management or whole-loan trading. Because the tools now exist to risk-stratify a portfolio of single-family whole loans periodically or to review the risk status and market value of the remaining loans supporting a previously issued security, a unique dimension has been added to mortgage analytics.

Phillip R. Pollock is a partner in Tobin & Tobin, PC, San Francisco. His clients include Redwood Trust, Inc.; NovaStar Financial, Inc.; American Residential Investment Trust, Inc.; SunAmerica Investments, Inc.; Headlands Mortgage Co., and Standard Financial Corp. Pollock represented Bank of America in the development and issuance of the first conventional mortgage pass-through security. He has represented issuers, underwriters, and others in a variety of mortgage-related financings as well as asset-backed securities.

Pollock joined Tobin & Tobin in 1995. Earlier, he was with Skadden, Arps, Slate, Meagher & Flom (1987-1995), Brown & Wood (1978-1986), Bank of America legal department (1976-1978), and Sullivan & Cromwell (1974-1976). His professional affiliations include the American Bar Association and the Mortgage Bankers Association of America.

Pollock holds a BA from Stanford University, an MBA from Stanford Graduate School of Business, and a JD from Stanford Law School.

Michael E. Shaff is a partner at Jeffers, Wilson, Shaff & Falk, LLP, Irvine, California, where he specializes in all aspects of federal income taxation. Shaff is co-author of the *Real Estate Investment Trusts Handbook* published by West Group.

His practice includes all aspects of REIT taxation, related finance transactions, and debt and equity offerings. Shaff co-founded the firm in 1994 after practicing tax law for the prior three years with Nordman, Cormany, Hair & Compton in Ventura County and for the previous five years with the New York firm of Kaye, Scholer, Fierman, Hays & Handler. Shaff also served as an attorney with the office of the Chief Counsel of the Internal Revenue Service for three years. He is certified by the Board of Legal Specialization of the State Bar of California as a specialist in taxation law. He is a member of the American Bar Association , the state bars of California, Massachusetts, and New York, and is current chair of the tax section of the Orange County Bar Association.

Shaff holds a BA degree from Columbia University and JD and LLM in Taxation degrees from New York University School of Law.

Chapter 10

FASIT Flexibility Applied to Subprime Securitizations

Phillip R. Pollock
Partner
Tobin & Tobin

Michael E. Shaff
Partner
Jeffers, Wilson, Shaff & Falk, LLP

The Financial Asset Securitization Investment Trust (FASIT) provides increased flexibility in structuring subprime asset securitizations. While the use of FASITs is not limited to subprime assets, the enhanced structuring possibilities created by FASITs can be important in maximizing the efficiency of subprime securitizations, from the issuer's standpoint. (Efficiency, for this purpose, can be measured by the relative amount of proceeds received by the issuer at closing from a given amount of collateral. The more efficient the transaction, relatively speaking, the more proceeds will be realized by the issuer and/or relatively lower levels of collateral will be required.)

Subprime assets generally possess two characteristics that limit the efficiency of securitizations. First, subprime assets by definition have higher risk of credit loss and, hence, require higher levels of credit support than prime-quality assets. Second, subprime assets have higher yields than prime assets, which creates "excess yield" that is usually required to be applied as additional credit support. FASITs can enhance the efficiency of subprime securitizations by reducing the required level of credit support in the form of initial overcollateralization and by reducing the amount of excess yield required to be applied to credit support by, among other things, permitting earlier release of collateral. These enhancements can result in the issuer receiving more proceeds, more quickly, compared with non-FASIT structures.

ALTERNATIVES AVAILABLE PRIOR TO FASITS

Before adoption of the FASIT legislation, the Small Business Job Protection Act of 1996 (effective September 1, 1997), there were essentially three structural categories available for securitizing subprime assets, all of which are still available. For certain subprime real estate mortgage loans, including subprime first-lien mortgages and home equity closed-end mortgages, there is the real estate mortgage investment conduit (REMIC) vehicle. For mortgage loans that do not qualify for REMICs — such as home equity lines of credit (HELOCs), high loan-to-value mortgage loans (125%) and progress installment construction loans — there are the grantor trust and "debt for tax" structures. Neither of these non-REMIC structures permits multiple maturity securities to be issued, due to the Taxable Mortgage Pool (TMP) rules. (The TMP rules effectively limit pass-through tax treatment for entities that issue tranched debt supported by real estate mortgage loans loans to REMICs and FASITs.) Finally, for nonmortgage subprime assets, there is the trust classified as a partnership structure coupled with issuance of debt securities. This structure permits issuance of multiple maturity securities, since the assets being securitized are not subject to the TMP rules.

In general, gain is recognized when the holder of the ownership interest transfers debt to a FASIT. The FASIT provisions of the Internal Revenue Code permit an entity that was in existence on August 31, 1997, and that was structured in a manner that would have permitted the entity to elect FASIT status (i.e., as a trust or partnership and whose underlying assets consist solely of debt, credit enhancements, and hedges) as a pre-effective-date FASIT. Gain is not recognized on the election of FASIT status by a pre-effective-date FASIT.

ADVANTAGES OF FASITS VERSUS TRUST AND DEBT FOR TAX STRUCTURES

Once FASIT regulations are promulgated, the FASIT structure will provide a measure of certainty of the tax treatment to be accorded a securitization, as opposed to the uncertainty present when relying on "partnership" and "debt" interpretations. This benefit, however, has been reduced by the adoption of the check-the-box tax regulations (the IRS's new, simplified system of selecting the classification of most types of entities for tax purposes).

A more significant advantage is that, for the category of subprime mortgage loans that do not qualify for REMIC treatment, FASITs permit issuance of multiple maturity securities. This ability to have multiple tranches of senior-subordinated, fast pay/slow pay securities permits more efficient pricing and more attractive overcollateralization and collateral release terms compared with the grantor trust or debt-for-tax structures. It may also create more alternatives in the type of credit support used, such as tranching versus use of bond insurance.

Outside of the mortgage securitization context where the TMP rules limit multiple maturity tranching to REMICs and FASITs, the FASIT structure does not generally provide any structural advantages over a trust (taxed as a partnership) issuing debt securities. Since this structure is available for most nonmortgage financial assets, the FASIT structure may be less attractive to issuers of nonmortgage securitizations solely from the standpoint of maximizing efficiency. There may be other reasons, however, for such issuers to adopt the FASIT structure provided that the disadvantages of using it are not significantly greater than the trust issuing debt for tax structure.

The most significant disadvantages presented by use of FASITs versus the trust or debt for tax approach are the recognition of gain required upon formation of FASITs and the possible recognition of "phantom" income over time by the holder of the ownership interest. A discussion of these tax treatments appears below.

ADVANTAGES OF FASITS VERSUS REMICS

A major benefit of FASITs over REMICs is the ability to add or substitute assets to the structure after the startup period and to remove collateral from the structure. This flexibility permits use of mortgage assets in a trust or other entity that issues fixed-term maturities, similar to credit card or other receivable securitizations.

Prior to FASITs, such fixed-term securities would have to meet tests for classification as debt for tax purposes and would be subject to the restrictions of the TMP rules. Under the REMIC and TMP rules, the REMIC originally was designated to be the sole vehicle for issuing multiple-maturity mortgage-backed debt. In the nonmortgage context there are no such restrictions.

Another advantage of FASITs over REMICs is that FASITs can hold a combination of qualifying mortgages along with other types of debt instruments. REMICs permit only qualifying mortgages, plus cash, reserves and related assets. An issuer can combine a pool of mortgage loans with interest rate agreements such as rate caps or floors to mitigate risks to the investors in the securities issued by a FASIT. Among the permitted assets that may be transferred to the FASIT are an interest rate or foreign currency notional principal contract, letter of credit, insurance contract, guarantee against payment defaults, or other financial contract reasonably required to guarantee or hedge against the FASIT's risks associated with being the obligor on interests issued by the FASIT, contract rights to acquire debt instruments, any regular interest in another FASIT, and any regular interest in a REMIC.

ILLUSTRATIVE EXAMPLE OF TWO-STEP FASIT STRUCTURE

To facilitate analysis and discussion of the tax treatment and public offering status of potential subprime FASIT securitizations, it will be helpful to set forth a sample structure. The structure posited for this purpose is based on the structure recently used in the first publicly offered FASIT securitization issued by American Residential Eagle, Inc., in June 1998. This two-step structure can be particularly advantageous to subprime issuers for the following reasons.

In this structure, the originator/seller transfers (via a sale transaction) to a special purpose, bankruptcy-remote subsidiary a pool of HELOCs (or any other financial assets). The special-purpose subsidiary (SPS) then pledges the HELOCs to secure the issuance of a HELOC bond, treated as debt for tax purposes. This HELOC bond (and any subsequently issued HELOC bonds backed by future HELOC originations or future advances) is referred to herein as the "underlying security" or "underlying bond." The initial overcollaterization required by the rating agencies can be put in place at this stage, as security for the underlying bond.

As the second step, the SPS transfers the HELOC bond (and any subsequently issued HELOC bonds) to a FASIT trust or a Wall Street conduit depositor for deposit into a FASIT trust. The FASIT trust issues trust certificates representing FASIT regular interests and any high-yield interests to the SPS as payment for the HELOC bond, and the trust certificates are sold to investors. The ownership interest is issued to a third-party investor or retained by the Wall Street depositor. The FASIT trust certificates sold to investors can be multiple-maturity, fast-pay/slow-pay, tranched securities, or fixed-term securities followed by a liquidation period or bullet maturity. Additional transfers to the FASIT trust (in the form of additional HELOC bonds) can be used to support issuance of new classes of FASIT certificates or to support outstanding classes of certificates.

This two-step structure, which ultimately depends on the cash flow from the pool of loans or receivables backing the HELOC bond, is an attractive structure to maximize efficiency of subprime asset securitizations. It permits mortgage loan securitizations to realize the benefits of

Chapter 10: FASIT Flexibility Applied to Subprime Securitizations

FASITs over the REMIC and debt for tax structures discussed above. It also permits any asset-backed FASIT securitization to mitigate the negative effects of the FASIT gain-on-sale provisions.

The two-step structure is a significant structural advantage of FASITs compared with REMICs and other forms of existing securitization structures. Because FASITs permit any instruments classified as debt for tax purposes as "permitted assets" it is possible to have an underlying bond or other underlying security as the permitted assets of a FASIT. This fact introduces the potential for the two-step and other creative structures which are not possible with REMICs, which permit only qualifying mortgages (and related items) as acceptable assets to back issuance of REMIC interests. The two-step structure has many potential applications in addition to the HELOC example described above, including the subprime mortgage loan FASIT offering completed by American Residential Eagle, Inc., in June 1998.

TAXATION OF SUBPRIME FASIT SECURITIZATIONS

Sponsor

As noted, the primary drawback of the FASIT structure is the requirement of gain (but not loss) recognition on the transfer of the debt obligations to the FASIT. When the sponsor transfers the HELOCs (or any other form of debt) to the trust that will elect FASIT status, gain is recognized. In the absence of regulations, the gain is computed by discounting the projected cash flows of the transferred debt at 120% of the applicable federal rate (AFR) published monthly by the IRS. The November 1998 rate that would likely apply to calculate gain in most situations is 5.42% (120% of AFR for instruments with terms of more than three but not more than nine years).

In the two-step structure described above, the sponsor issues its own debt instrument. The sponsor generally will not have to recognize gain on the issuance of its own debt, but there will be tax implications for both the sponsor and the holder of the FASIT ownership interest.

Where the sponsor is a C corporation, it may retain the ownership interest in the FASIT. If the sponsor is a real estate investment trust (REIT), partnership, or other passthrough entity, it is ineligible to hold the ownership interest. The debt instruments that will be the assets of the FASIT are deemed sold to the entity that will hold the ownership interest.

Holders

Holders of regular FASIT interests are treated as holding debt. Regular interests yield no more than 5% above the AFR at the time of issuance. High-yield instruments (yielding more than 5% over the AFR, having a term longer than 30 years, or issued at a premium of more than 25% over the interest's stated principal) may be held only by a C corporation or by a dealer who acquires them for resale. The holder of a FASIT interest must use the accrual method for income from the FASIT interest. Where the holder is a REIT, the FASIT regular interest is a qualifying real estate asset where at least 95% of the FASIT's loans are mortgage loans secured by real estate. REITs and regulated investment companies (RICs) are not eligible to hold high yield FASIT interests. (The high-yield subordinated regular interests of a REMIC could be transferred to a REIT or RIC.) If the FASIT trust holds mortgages and not collateralized mortgage obligations (CMOs), the FASIT interests in one of the two highest rating categories should be "mortgage related securities" for depository institutions.

Owner

A FASIT is permitted to have only one ownership interest, which must be held by a C corporation. The FASIT's assets and liabilities, and items of income, gain, loss, deduction, or credit pass through to the holder of this ownership interest. All assets transferred to the FASIT are deemed sold to the holder of the ownership interest. The holder of the ownership interest includes in income all of the FASIT's income net of deductions for interest and original issue discount accruing on the regular interests. The owner may not offset the FASIT income by the holder's net operating loss.

IMPEDIMENTS UNDER CURRENT SEC RULES TO USE OF FASIT STRUCTURES IN PUBLIC OFFERINGS

Registration Form Problems

Right to Use Form S-3 Form S-3 is available to certain types of issuers and securities that satisfy the criteria set forth in the form. Use of Form S-3 is important because it provides for incorporation by reference of certain information filed by the issuer pursuant to other public reporting provisions, and it permits "shelf" registration of securities to be issued

Chapter 10: FASIT Flexibility Applied to Subprime Securitizations

from time to time up to two years following registration. The ability to use shelf registration is important to securitization issuers because the SEC does not review the shelf "takedowns" after its initial review of the registration upon filing. Hence, the timing of conducting a takedown offering is largely in the control of the issuer and is not subject to the uncertainties of timing that result from SEC review.

Form S-3 was revised in 1992 to permit use by issuers of asset-backed securities, provided certain criteria are met. If such criteria are not met, the only alternatives are (1) to file separately for each offering (with possible SEC review) or (2) if the assets being securitized are mortgage loans and satisfy the criteria for issuance of "mortgage related" securities (including first-lien status), shelf registration is available under Rule 415 for any classes of securities rated in the two highest rating categories. (Form S-3 permits classes that are "investment grade," which includes the four highest rating categories.)

Discrete Pool Requirement To be eligible for Form S-3, the securities to be issued must be primarily serviced by the cashflows of a discrete pool of receivables or other financial assets, either fixed or revolving. The SEC release that accompanied the 1992 revisions to Form S-3 pointed out that the reference to "fixed or revolving" was added to make clear that revolving-balance financial assets, such as credit card receivables, were acceptable assets to be offered on Form S-3. The staff reached this conclusion while pointing out that, depending on the performance of the revolving assets included in a discrete pool, "the sponsor may be required to assign additional receivables from other accounts" to support the outstanding securities. The addition of other accounts in such circumstances apparently does not impair the original discrete-pool status.

The SEC staff now takes the position that the addition of assets to a FASIT pool, as well as the substitution or removal of assets from a pool, would violate the discrete pool requirement and hence the securities offered in such a FASIT structure would not qualify for Form S-3. This position requires FASIT issuers to forego the FASIT flexibility for adding and removing assets if Form S-3 is used.

Asset Concentration Requirement Another requirement that must be met to be eligible for the "asset backed" security provisions of Form S-3 is that a pool of assets must be present so that the cashflows supporting the asset-backed security do not depend on a single or a limited number of sources but, rather, on a large number of obligors. Under the current SEC view, if the securities of a single obligor or group of related obligors comprise 45% or more of the pool, the asset-backed security provisions of

Form S-3 are not available.

For purposes of this requirement, the SEC staff does not look through a security to the underlying source of payments due on the security. Hence, in the HELOC example or any other two-step structure, even though the underlying bond is wholly supported by and dependent solely on the underlying pool of HELOC mortgage loans, the structure is not eligible for Form S-3. This refusal to look through to the underlying source of payments supporting an asset-backed security is also a problem for single obligor commercial securitizations where the underlying source of payments comprises a pool of retail leases or other small obligations of unrelated obligors.

Convert into Cash Requirement To qualify as an asset-backed security, the underlying assets must also "by their terms convert into cash within a finite time period." The SEC staff interprets this requirement as excluding any loans or receivables that are nonperforming (in foreclosure or nonaccrual status) and as permitting no more than 20% of a pool to be delinquent at the date of securities issuance. These limitations make Form S-3 unavailable to certain types of subprime securitizations, such as tax lien pools, real estate owned (REO) pools, and workout loan pools.

Multiple Core Prospectus Requirement The SEC staff made clear in adopting the revisions to Form S-3 that the prospective disclosure in the core prospectus, reviewed by the staff, must be detailed and complete as to each type of asset to be securitized. "A registration statement may not merely identify several alternative types of assets that may be securitized."

This view of the staff is also applied without "looking through" to the ultimate source of payments. In the HELOC example, and any other two-step structure, the staff regards the underlying bond or other underlying security as a type of asset to be fully described in the core prospectus. Hence, a core prospectus that described HELOCs (as opposed to the underlying bond) would be unacceptable for purposes of offering the FASIT trust certificates in the HELOC example. This approach virtually precludes the use of Wall Street conduits to securitize an underlying bond or other security in a two-step structure because no conduit shelf will have anticipated such underlying securities as a type of asset to be described.

Furthermore, the SEC staff requires that separate core prospectuses be filed if the type of asset to be securitized is so different from other types covered by the core prospectus that a full description requires separate treatment (such as separate risk factors section, description of terms, etc.). This approach can lead to unwieldy multiple prospectuses that are more likely to discourage the reader than to inform, even in the age of "plain English."

Co-Issuer Problems

Single Obligor Requirement Under present SEC staff interpretations, if the securities of a single obligor or group of related obligors comprise 45% or more of the pool, then such obligor or obligors may be deemed co-issuers required to file a registration statement covering such underlying securities, and to deliver a prospectus covering such underlying securities, along with the prospectus covering the securities being sold to investors. The only exceptions to this rule are (1) if the underlying securities have been registered and sold (in a valid secondary market sale) more than three months prior to the current securitization and (2) if the underlying securities were privately issued and sold more than two years prior to the current securitization (such that Rule 144(k) would apply). The underlying security in the HELOC example and other two-step structures will not fit within these exceptions and hence will be subject to compliance with the co-issuer rules.

Co-Issuer Form Problems One major problem posed by the co-issuer interpretation is that the underlying security registration is subject to the same registration form requirements as the securities being sold to investors. Accordingly, even where using a Wall Street conduit that permits an underlying security of the type used in the HELOC or other two-step structure, since the underlying bond or the security will fail to satisfy one or more of the above Form S-3 criteria, each offering will fail the Form S-3 criteria and will have to be separately registered.

Multiple Core and/or Supplemental Prospectus Requirement To satisfy the SEC staff interpretation that both the securities being sold to investors and the underlying security are being offered and sold in a two-step structure, it may be necessary to have two separate core prospectuses and two separate prospectus supplements. The SEC staff is agreeable to combined core and/or supplemental prospectuses where one issuer can control the disclosure and describe fully in one document each security covered thereby. However, this flexibility is not present where, for example, a Wall Street shelf is being used to issue a separately registered security of an unaffiliated issuer. This situation can require multiple core and supplemental prospectuses that do not serve to inform investors in a meaningful way due to overlapping, duplicative disclosure and the sheer mass of the disclosure document itself.

Multiple Filing Fees A further impediment to a public offering involving a co-issuer structure is that the SEC staff currently takes the position that two separate filing fees are required. This results in what is, in effect, a double filing fee for each dollar of proceeds raised from investors, compared with a non-two-step structure.

Mallory P. Hill is managing director of Mortgages PLC, a leading U.K. subprime lender. The company was created when Hill and J. Todd Morley, chairman of Links Securities LLC, formed a joint venture with the principals of a highly regarded U.K. mortgage packager, The Mortgage Operation. Paul Marks, Trevor Pothecary, and Frank Butler have combined experience of over 70 years in the U.K. real estate finance industry.

With Merrill Lynch as the original working-capital and warehouse provider, the company has become one of the top four volume originators of subprime mortgages in the United Kingdom. Mortgages PLC, the "all-status" lender, has originated nearly £100 million in the first year since its product launch in March 1998. The company has a highly skilled team of seasoned industry professionals led by Paul Thomas, chief operating officer.

Hill has many years of experience in real estate finance, over 10 on Wall Street. During nine years at Donaldson, Lufkin & Jenrette, he focused on principal mortgage finance. He was responsible for the creation of the first subprime/Wall Street joint venture, Quality Mortgage. He was actively involved in the origination, securitization, and sale of several billion dollars of nonstandard mortgage product.

Prior to Wall Street, Hill was a top producer in commercial sales and leasing for a large national real estate firm, Arthur Rubloff & Co. He now divides his time between London and his home base in California, where he owns and operates mortgage-related companies: Beneficial Capital Management, American Interstate Credit, American Interstate Escrow, and New Life Funding.

Mortgages PLC intends to continue its business success and market efficiencies with growth into other countries on the European continent as well as growth into other types of mortgage products.

Hill is a graduate of the University of California at Berkeley, where he studied economics and business.

Chapter 11

Evolution of Subprime Mortgage Lending in the United Kingdom

Mallory P. Hill
Managing Director
Mortgages PLC

The U.K. mortgage market is becoming a more noticeable blip on the radar screens watched closely by Wall Street, North American financial companies, and institutional investors. The reasons are many for this increased visibility in recent years. As a natural outgrowth of mortgage finance as conducted in North America and the efficient market developed there, the United Kingdom represents growth opportunities due to a number of factors, including its proximity to Europe.

The United Kingdom has a diversified economy with a substantial population approaching 60 million. Home-ownership levels are relatively high compared with other developed countries, and the level, currently 65%, continues to grow. The demographics of U.K. consumers bode positively for lenders as consumption and related debt levels increase, as has been the case with U.S. consumers. As asset-backed lenders, the subprime industry is especially focused on the value of the homes being borrowed against. The timing appears good in the United Kingdom, as values today represent a relative low point in the real estate valuation cycle. With a common language and lender-friendly laws, the United Kingdom beckons U.S. mortgage finance companies seeking additional markets abroad.

In the context of asset-based lending, the subprime mortgage sector, already established in the United States, has focused actively on the U.K. market's potential since 1996. The timing, following a period of recession and with rising but relatively low real estate values, has strengthened the appeal for participation in the United Kingdom.

GATEWAY TO EUROPE: 240 MILLION POTENTIAL CUSTOMERS

The 11-nation European Monetary Union officially introduced the euro in January 1999. This common currency will change the way Western Europe conducts business, and the new "United States of Europe" is surely poised for economic growth that will present many opportunities. For example, the European home-ownership rate is well below that of the United States at present. U.S. mortgage-banking efficiencies could well be used to finance any potential increase in that rate. The single currency will ultimately increase liquidity and volume, and improve existing European mortgage secondary markets.

This chapter discusses the residential mortgage market in the United Kingdom, beginning with a brief history of the events that led to the forays made by Wall Street in the 1980s and again more particularly into subprime in the 1990s. It also addresses some of the issues regarding the players within this industry and the regulatory/political climate that will no doubt impact upon the manner in which business is conducted in the future.

THE MARKET: AN HISTORICAL PERSPECTIVE

In order to comprehend the subprime market, one must first understand the primary market and recognize that most subprime loans are based on prime underwriting standards, adjusted for risk.

The mortgage market in the United Kingdom has for decades been dominated by the building societies and, since the 1980s, by the major banks. The building societies (much like U.S. mutuals and savings & loans) generated a majority of their total assets in the category of residential mortgages. The larger players in these groups had oligopolies of sorts; and the barriers to entry remain high today. In fact, prime or "status" business has recently been priced inside of where equivalent U.S. liabilities would be written in many cases.

For example, prime borrowers in the United Kingdom can today execute a three-year, fixed-rate loan at around 4.5% and a five-year at or below 6%. In the United States these would be priced off the corresponding Treasury curve, which in May 1999 was 5.40% three years, 5.48% five years. In terms of the London interbank offered rate (LIBOR), 5.45% was the corresponding three-month rate in May 1999. In all cases, U.S. liabilities would be priced at the index or curve plus 100 basis points, at minimum. One can see, therefore, how competitive the pricing is on prime mortgage business. On its face — from the outsider's point of view — not a profitable place to write business.

The balance sheets of these institutions are much like those of their U.S. counterparts prior to the decade 1980-1990: long-term assets in the form of mortgages (first charges) against residential properties, with offsetting liabilities of shorter-term customer deposits and other financings.

To look more closely at the size of the U.K. mortgage market and the respective size of the credit-impaired market, one must extrapolate. The current U.K. mortgage market is approximately £89 billion, or $150 billion, in gross advances each year. For example, in 1996 the figure stood at £71,246 million. The total outstanding balances through July 1997 were approximately £421 billion. The estimated size of the nonconforming market in terms of gross advances is considered to be in the region of 20% of the total. Therefore, the potential size of the nonconforming/credit-impaired market can be estimated to be in the region of £17.8 billion ($30 billion) per annum in terms of gross advances or approximately £90 billion ($153 billion) in terms of total outstanding balances.

The primary difference between the two countries' mortgage books has been the high percentage of fixed-rate loans among U.S. institutions. According to the U.K.'s Council of Mortgage Lenders, fixed-rate loans still account for a little more than 55% of all loans, although this has almost doubled since the early 1990s. In the United States, this asset-liability mismatch created by funding long-term assets with short-term liabilities has bedeviled myriad bank executives, especially in periods of inverted yield curves. The U.K. market has historically benefited from a mortgage asset that is variable-rate and therefore better matched to its corresponding liability. Standard variable rate (SVR) is the market norm among U.K. lenders, although, in recent years, lenders have been driven to offer shorter-term fixed rates to write business in an increasingly competitive environment. SVR is managed much like the commercial prime rate in the United States. In practice, the rate tends to move up more rapidly than it moves down. Of interest, these movements have customarily been in favor of the lender.

The traditional leaders, the building societies, have enjoyed the benefit of sourcing funds to lend from both their retail savers and from the money markets. At any given point, they calculate their blended cost of funds, and price above that accordingly — which can give them greater flexibility in pricing, especially at times when interest rates are high in the United Kingdom. Rates paid to savers are historically lower than money market rates, which has enabled the societies to hold back on the most severe price increases on mortgages.

However, as U.K. rates reduce ahead of potential convergence with the euro, some market observers believe the societies may find it difficult to attract retail deposits to the same degree going forward. Nevertheless, managing a mortgage book with a substantial element of SVR-based loans has enabled many prime U.K. lenders to secure new business in a competitive environment by offering attractive short-term fixed or capped rates, or lead-in discounts and/or cashbacks, together with extended prepayment penalties, which revert to SVR after the honeymoon period. Mortgage amortization and terms are largely 25 years (versus 30 years in the United States), or 25 years with a five-year or 10-year balloon. In some cases, lenders offer interest-only loans to prime borrowers, with our without the requirement for assignable life cover.

Particularly since the mid-1980s, mortgage distribution in the United Kingdom has been strongly influenced by financial services intermediaries (typically, independent financial advisers, mortgage brokers, and life insurance company salesmen). Intermediary mortgage distribution was boosted when certain American and European banks — Citibank, Chemical Bank, CIBC, and BNP, for example — entered the U.K. market and identified this channel as more cost-effective than going directly to the public. Fierce competition among traditional lenders and the new, centralized (that is, branchless) lenders stimulated product innovation for the first time in the United Kingdom and firmly established the intermediary channel.

While no exact statistics are available, somewhere between 50% and 60% of new mortgage business is currently originated through financial advisers, who are usually able to offer clients a choice of mortgage types and lenders. There are currently some 70 building societies and 70 other lending institutions in the United Kingdom, although a relatively small number account for the lion's share of lending by value.

The U.K. product type is somewhat different from what is seen in the U.S. market, where an average loan-to-value ratio might be 75% — with 80% maximum on standard prime. U.K. lenders have for years written a healthy percentage of their loans at 90% to 95% maximum LTV; some programs have lent 100% LTV to assist first-time buyers. This higher LTV has been offset by U.K. features such as direct debit payments, mandatory life-insurance cover (with the lender named as the beneficiary in the event of death during the life of the loan), and by mortgage indemnity guarantee insurance covering loss of sale on high-LTV loans. Many borrowers also have mortgage payment policies that cover loss of job. Currently, however, intense competition is diluting some of these requirements; some lenders have reduced or waived portions of them. In any event, the market expects a higher-LTV product and, to date, the subprime players have met this expectation with some higher-LTV products to 95% loan-to-value ratio.

Traditional underwriting by U.K. lenders would look to typical industry standards such as length of employment, debt-to-income ratios, and clean credit history. Credit history is an issue that presents structural or qualitative differences from the U.S. market. At present, credit reporting is not as developed in the United Kingdom. Information on bor-

Chapter 11: Evolution of Subprime Mortgage Lending in the U.K.

rowers is shared among some lenders but not to the extent of Fair Isaac Co. (FICO)-type credit scoring, shared information a la TRW and other credit-reporting agencies in the United States. However, there are two major credit-reference agencies that record debt judgments, credit defaults, and residency. Additionally, the appraisal process in the United Kingdom represents a qualitative upgrade from its U.S. analogy. "Chartered surveyors" in the U.K. are bonded and liable financially in the event of negligent valuations.

All of the U.K. first-mortgage lenders deal with either Experian or Equifax or both. These agencies will generally decline or, at the least, scrutinize applications very closely if there is a record of adverse credit or insufficient proof of residency. A county court judgment, or CCJ, is the official derogatory. Building societies, for instance, strictly limit the degree to which they will proceed with applicants who have had a number of CCJs, or where the value of one or more CCJs exceeds a finite sum such as £500. This is because such borrowers fall into the category of higher-risk lending for the building societies.

CCJs recorded against borrowers will be extinguished from their credit records six years after initial date of registration — irrespective of whether they have been satisfied. There are around one million CCJs issued year, of which 2,000 to 3,000 are satisfied each week, or 130,000 to 150,000 each year. Once an underwriting decision is made to deny credit, the borrower was forced to look to subprime — or nonstatus — lenders, as is the case in the United States. Some institutions dabbled quietly in portfolio or quasi-prime mortgages in exchange for higher interest rates and/or lower loan-to-value ratios.

In the mid- to late 1980s, a number of new, "centralized" lenders (that is, specialists funded via the money market) wrote A-type paper. Included in this category were The Mortgage Corporation, Hypo Bank, Household Mortgage Corporation, and National Home Loans. These lenders were more flexible with regard to proofs of status and income multiples and generally wrote a lower average LTV to mitigate risk.

A new criterion was introduced by the evolving U.K. centralized lender, the self-certification of income, or limited-status, lending. This criterion became popular as a result of competition and the short-term view at that time that values would not stop rising. Lenders stretched their LTVs to 80% readily for those loans and were protected by little more than this ratio other than their credit search, valuation and, in some cases, previous lender's reference. Self-certification is much like "stated income" in the United States, for which applicants need to state (or certify) only their income and occupation. This facility is mainly offered to self-employed borrowers.

In practice, some of these lenders were more prudent than others. But all were at a severe disadvantage to established traditional lenders when the property market recession hit, because they held immature books all initiated from the mid-'80s. As a result, equity protection was reduced as the market value of properties dropped from 1991 through 1994 by up to 50% in some areas.

Other than these quasi-prime lenders, once potential borrowers were denied loans by an A-lender, the availability of options boiled down to consumer finance companies, as in the United States. Those companies were actually many of the same players that most people in the U.S. industry were familiar with: Household, AVCO, Associates, to name a few. These operations have been writing business in the United Kingdom since the 1960s and 1970s.

For the consumer finance company in the U.K., business has until recently had one large advantage over the United States: the Rule of 78. This law permitted the lender to charge the borrower the entire amount of finance charges due under the full term of the loan — regardless of whether the loan was paid off in advance of schedule or lasted the entire term of 10-15-25 years. This was "the ultimate prepayment penalty." Supposedly, it compensated the lender for opportunity lost — being paid less than expected. The lender's inducement to make the original loan, after all, was a calculation based on the total profit.

As is the case in North America, finance company rates of interest can easily run to 15% to 20% per annum, with some firms charging origination points and fees of up to 10% or 20% of the loan balance. In the United States in the 1970s these were called "vision loans" — as in 20/20!

With these rates of interest, one can see that the net present value (NPV) at loan payoff would be very expensive for any borrower who prepaid. As mentioned previously, this type of portfolio loan was kept on the balance sheet and a portion of the excess coupon would be used to reserve against expected losses. Earnings were generated over the life of the loan, as the borrowers made their scheduled payments.

DISTRIBUTION

Distribution of mortgage product at the retail level is accomplished in the United Kingdom by mortgage brokers and independent financial advisors (IFAs). They are fee- and commission-based operators, usually on a local or regional basis. Wholesale distribution is provided by packagers, which gather their production through developed networks of mortgage brokers and IFAs. Packagers submit completed packages to the lenders and are paid a fee/commission if a loan is ultimately made. As in the

United States, true retail lending by the building societies and banks is also sourced through their retail branches.

Intermediary mortgage distribution is generally fragmented; there are currently around 35,000 individuals registered with the Mortgage Code Register of Intermediaries (MCRI) and permitted to give mortgage advice. However, during the 1990s a new breed of mortgage "wholesaler" has evolved. These organizations act as a conduit between the lenders and the point-of-sale mortgage advisers, offering efficiency of loan distribution for lenders and ease of access to product selection for intermediaries. There are several of these, the most notable being The Mortgage Operation PLC, which is now the largest independent distributor of mortgage through intermediaries, with its nationwide network of some 3,000 mortgage adviser members (who pay a subscription for the service, which includes the mortgage-sourcing software offering hundreds of products ranging in price from nonconforming through subprime.)

EXCESS(IVE) INTEREST: ENTER U.S. SUBPRIME PLAYERS

The development of the securitization market in the U.S. capital markets in the late 1980s and early 1990s supercharged earnings of some U.S. mortgage and finance companies by allowing loan originators to take the upfront gain-on-sale and remove the loans from their balance sheets by selling the mortgage assets and securitizing them. The major point of interest is that this mortgage-backed securitization allowed aggressive growth of the subprime asset type — far more, in fact, than the typical portfolio lender would achieve on its traditional balance sheet.

In the United States, these "efficiencies" of Wall Street and the unique ruling of gain-on-sale by the Financial Accounting Standards Board worked together to create a huge market for B and C (subprime) paper in securitized form. One U.S.-based company, Cityscape Mortgage of New York, came to the United Kingdom in March 1995 and put the principles of the Rule of 78 to work with the net-present-value efficiencies of the mortgage securitization market. Cityscape subsequently purchased two U.K.-based corporations, J&J and Heritable and their respective subprime mortgage books. Utilizing the Rule of 78 and dual interest rates (whereby delinquent borrowers' coupons were raised punitively by as much as 7% to 10%), Cityscape brought to market a mortgage securitization in 1996 that attracted serious interest from North America. Excessive gains (far greater than 10 points) could be imputed using the senior subordinated structure that Wall Street had successfully executed to the tune of hundreds of billions of dollars.

WHITE-HOT FOCUS

Once the prospectus from the Cityscape deal hit the desks of mortgage players, the invasion from North America began in earnest. The summer of 1996 saw most of the U.S.-based subprime companies examining the U.K. market, with many vowing to become active originators. The attention of Wall Street to the aspect of "punitive consumer pricing structure" was followed by the scrutiny of the British press and the Office of Fair Trading. Of particular interest was Cityscape's *modus operandi*. Were British citizens being taken advantage of? Since that time, a number of companies have set up shop in the U.K subprime market. Some have come and gone, others persist with degrees of success, while some thrive. Reasons for the varying degrees of success enjoyed by their efforts will be examined in the following sections on the structure of the market, the major players, and product types, and, lastly, on securitization in the United Kingdom.

STRUCTURE

The Council of Mortgage Lenders (CML) supervises the entire first-mortgage market in the United Kingdom. CML is a trade body made up of lender members — constituents who subscribe to the council and agree to abide by its rules and good practice in lending. These rules are embodied in the CML's Code of Mortgage Lending Practice, which applies to both lenders and intermediaries; but, as of date of publication of this book, there is no regulatory or legislative force behind it.

However, legislation may be on the horizon when the Financial Services Authority (FSA) turns its attention to the mortgage market. The FSA is at the heart of the new structure for financial regulation in the United Kingdom and is currently undertaking a major exercise in progressively managing and absorbing the diverse financial services areas of activity.

CML's duty to self-regulate became more prominent with the attention focused on Cityscape by the media and the Office of Fair Trading (OFT). Of most concern to them was the Rule of 78; the heavy cost to borrowers of dual pricing and prepayment penalties; and the excessive fees paid to brokers — all of which were applied to borrowers who were by definition vulnerable because of their circumstances.

The Council of Mortgage Lenders counts as its members the majority of the building societies, commercial bankers, and centralized lenders. Not all subprime lenders are members of the council, but the major players — including Kensington and Mortgages PLC — have joined.

As discussed in the historical perspective, the subprime industry

Chapter 11: Evolution of Subprime Mortgage Lending in the U.K.

in the United Kingdom is quite distinct from the majority of mainstream prime lenders. The large commercial banks and building societies dominate the prime or "status" market. Unlike the U.S. mortgage market, credit information and borrowers' credit history in the United Kingdom is not necessarily a public commodity. The major lenders can share information among themselves; the standards are unlike those in the United States wherein a number of credit bureaus are available to cross-reference reportable information. Similarly, there is no industrywide credit-scoring agency such as Fair Isaac. Underwriting in the United Kingdom is based upon credit derogatories (as reported or verifiable), debt/income multiples, employment (and length thereof), and loan-to-value ratio.

Also mentioned previously, CCJs (county court judgments) are the most reported form of derogatory credits. These range from unpaid domestic utility bills to disputed business or private debts. Most subprime originators allow a number of CCJs, whereas prime lenders generally find these unacceptable.

Essentially, underwriters are charged with deciphering the likelihood of payment by a borrower based upon the information at hand. Intelligent and experienced lenders have done this type of business for many decades. Having the largest balance sheet doesn't necessarily make one the best or brightest or most profitable. Volume in the United Kingdom to date – in the spirit of the "pump up the volume" U.S. gain-on-sale of the 1990s — has not been the important measure. Here, earnings accrue over the life of the loan (net of reserves); one must argue that the only loans that should be written are those that are likely to pay over time. This old-time discipline has recently been forced on many players in the U.S. market, as fewer and fewer U.S. players are using gain-on-sale accounting.

UK SUBPRIME LENDERS

The gap between prime lenders and the old-line consumer finance companies has been filled in the last few years by true subprime mortgage finance companies that originate first mortgages with expanded underwriting guidelines.

The first high-profile U.K. subprime lender was Kensington Mortgage Company, launched with U.K. and U.S. private funding in early 1996. In the following two years, Preferred, Future, Southern Pacific, Money Store, Mortgages PLC, and RFC all came on to the scene — thus creating a highly active and competitive market sector which, by definition, did not exist before. Its rapid development was assisted by the readiness of the U.K. market for "fresh start" facilities following the severe property recession of the early 1990s. That is to say, the last recession created — or expanded — a large class of borrowers with previous credit derogatories.

Cityscape's City Mortgage Corporation (CMC) had been operating prior to Kensington, but on a relatively low-profile basis, and obtained its distribution largely through secured-loan or second-mortgage brokers, unlike the new lenders who operate in the main broker markets. Of note is that CMC was purchased by Ocwen, which is now lending actively — mainly in CMS's traditional distribution channel, but without the Rule of 78 or dual pricing that had caused much consternation among the press and regulatory bodies. All of the subprime players today lend without the Rule of 78.

PRODUCTS

The first subprime products offered by the new breed of specialist lender since 1996 have been priced based on a margin over U.K. three-month LIBOR, depending on the perceived risk, and reset quarterly.

This is still the case, although two such lenders (Mortgages PLC and KMC) have introduced the concept of standard variable rate into this area of the market, Mortgages PLC innovated with SVR across its product line at launch in early 1998; Kensington followed in the same year.

As the subprime sector has grown, competition for market share has intensified with the consequence that product construction and pricing have become both more imaginative and aggressive. For instance, short-term, discounted, fixed and capped rates have been introduced as have accelerated service standards.

When the lenders first entered the U.K. market, initial pricing was not so much an issue. They sold on facility; that is, by offering to accommodate applicants regarded as nonconforming by the prime lenders; in other words, borrowers with an historical or current adverse credit history, providing they could satisfy the essential requirement that they would be both willing and able to service their mortgage now. These included recently self-employed applicants and those wishing to purchase or remortgage residential investment property. All of the subprime lenders also offer a self-certification facility subject to a more conservative loan-to-value upper limit.

Prepayment penalties have at the same time hardened, but not to the extent of the Rule of 78, which has now effectively been outlawed by the Office of Fair Trading for the U.K. subprime lenders. Also forbidden going forward is onerous dual-level pricing in the event of payment default. At present, prepayment penalties in the market usually range

Chapter 11: Evolution of Subprime Mortgage Lending in the U.K.

from three months' to six months' interest for just the first three to five years of the loan. Margin, after any concessionary initial period, usually ranges from 3% to 5% over three-month LIBOR or U.K. clearing bank base rate.

SECONDARY MARKETS/SECURITIES EXECUTION

Since the 1980s the U.K. market has employed Wall Street-type securitizations to varying degrees. The building societies and commercial banks do buy and sell whole-loan mortgage pools, but these are often private transactions that are by definition difficult to track.

Mortgage-backed securities issuance has averaged approximately £2 billion annually from 1988 onward. The "nonconforming/subprime" portion of this market really appeared in 1996 and grew to £1.25 billion issuance in 1998. As of May 1, 1999, over £600 million had been issued with another £600 million in line to be issued within the following three months. At this pace, 1999 will be the year in which subprime market issuance exceeds £2 billion. This is clearly a growth trajectory, as shown in Exhibit 1.

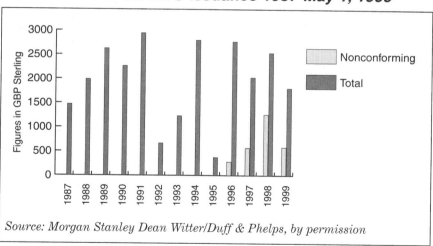

Exhibit 1: UK MBS Issuance 1987-May 1, 1999

Source: Morgan Stanley Dean Witter/Duff & Phelps, by permission

As with developing over-the-counter markets, increased production and issuance should lead to a more efficient market, with better pricing for issuers a likely byproduct.

Barclays Capital, an active market-maker in this sector, is

presently lead managing a number of new deals on behalf of some of the major issuers. Marc Bajer, director, believes this to be an improving market. According to Bajer, increased volume should aid the rating agencies in improving their models. More historical and issuer data from a wider field may lead to the following benefits:

- Tightening of loss assumptions for default frequency and severity.
- Excess spread and other credit enhancements, through greater use, may be valued more accurately.
- Reduction of total credit enhancement levels, which ultimately implies better pricing for issuers.
- Reduction in other related transaction costs as we have seen in the U.S. market, such as legal and accountancy fees.
- Expansion of product ranges for subprime borrowers.

OUTLOOK: YEAR 2000 AND BEYOND

Based upon the volumes of production and MBS issuance we will see for 1999, it is fair to say subprime finance is on a path of growth within the United Kingdom.

Interest rates are trending downward. The Bank of England cut its benchmark rate seven times between September 1998 and May 1999, to 5.0% from 7.5%, given a weak economy and fear of a recession. However, the economy has shown signs of bottoming out. Fourth-quarter 1998 showed barely any growth, but first-quarter 1999 showed signs of renewed growth. Many analysts are upping their forecasts closer to the government's 1999 projection of 1% to 1.5% growth. Inflation is expected to remain at the Monetary Policy Committee's target of 2.5% for the remainder of 1999. Considering the European Central Bank policy rate of 2.5%, a lower move in U.K. rates is a distinct possibility.

This positive rate outlook is complemented by a strong real estate market at present. Morgan Stanley's U.K. economist, Kevin Gardiner, predicts the Halifax House Price Index will shown price ranges of approximately 5% in 1999 and a further 4% in the year 2000. We have already seen this amount of appreciation in first-quarter 1999 for some regions.

The end game for the major players in this market amounts to good, judicious application of common sense. That is, price for risk and make loans in which the lender has a strong likelihood of recovery in the event of default by the borrower.

With increased regulatory scrutiny a near certainty, lenders must act fairly and in accordance with CML guidelines. I believe this

Chapter 11: Evolution of Subprime Mortgage Lending in the U.K.

market going forward will have a handful of major players competing for profit and market share based on time-honored business tenets: service, product innovation, pricing, and solid underwriting/risk management.

Index

A
abandon rate, 82
aftermarket product, 127
amortization, 104, 132, 170
applicable federal rate (AFR), 159-160
appraised value, 135
asset (backed) securitization, 40, 78, 86, 96, 128, 130, 138-140, 154-155, 159, 161-162, 167
asset-based lending, 167

B
balloon payment, 132
break-even pricing, 25
bucketing, 146
building society, 168-171, 173-175, 177
buyback, 122

C
capital adequacy, 19
capitalization, 127
chargeoff, 84, 90, 93
"chop," 126
collection, 17, 26-27, 29-30, 32-39, 46, 83-84, 90-92, 94, 100, 102, 109-110, 124, 133
commercial paper (CP) conduit, 115, 138, 156, 158, 162-163, 173
cost of funds, 104
Council of Mortgage Lenders (CML), 174
coupon rate, 104
covariance matrix, 60
credit
  gradient, 105
  impairment, 97
  modeling, 41, 44, 47-48, 56, 66-68
  niche, 105
  scoring, 41, 43-45, 47, 49, 51, 53, 55-59, 61-63, 65, 67, 69, 71, 73, 75-77, 81, 86, 100, 120, 134, 171

creditworthiness, 4-10, 12, 41-43, 62, 95, 109

D
data mining, 61, 65, 73, 76-77
debt-to-income ratio, 9, 23, 65
delinquency, 8, 10, 16-17, 22, 26-27, 37-38, 73, 83-84, 95, 110, 127, 134-136
derogatory, 175-176
dilution, 15, 18
discrete pool, 161
due diligence, 5, 14
duration, 18-19, 103-104

E
eigenvalue, 60, 70-71
Equifax, 171
equity sweetener, 114
European Monetary Union, 167
Experian, 171

F
factor-weighting, 70
Fair Isaac Co. (FICO), 86, 100, 120, 147-149, 171, 175
"false alarm," 45-46
fees, 80, 84, 89, 91, 93-94, 104, 114, 116, 126, 148, 151, 164, 172, 174, 178
Financial Accounting Standards Board (FASB), 108, 173
financial asset securitization investment trust (FASIT), 155-157, 159
Financial Services Authority (FSA), 174
first-month payment, 72
fixed term, 157-158
"flight to quality", 139
foreclosure, 18, 29, 31, 135, 148, 162
fraud detection, 81

Index

G
gain on sale, 18, 20, 107-108, 159, 173, 175
Generally Accepted Accounting Principles (GAAP), 107, 141

H
HELOC
home-equity
  loans (HELs), 131-133, 137-138, 140, 142
  HEL, adjustable-rate (ARM), 133
  lines of credit (HELOCs), 132, 158-159, 162-163

I
index, floating, 140
interest-only (IO) strip, 150-151
intermediary, 170, 173-174

L
LEVELS™, 24, 26, 42, 65, 82, 94, 120, 125, 134-135, 142, 147-150, 155, 167, 178
linear discriminant function, 50, 54
liquidation, 128, 148, 158
liquidity, 72, 104-105, 111, 113, 115-116, 140, 149, 168
Liquidity Crisis of 1998, 140
litigation, 18, 108, 128
loan-to-value (LTV) ratio, 18, 102-103, 124, 130, 133-136, 156, 170-171, 175-176
loss severity, 8, 10, 12, 17-18, 20, 22, 26, 100, 103, 132, 148

M
manufacturer's suggested retail price (MSRP), 129
mapping, 47, 59-60, 149
monoline enhancement, 115
monotonicity, 61, 65

Mortgage Code Register of Intermediaries (MCRI), 173
mortgage-backed securitization (MBS), 151, 173, 177-178

N
National Association of Insurance Commissioners (NAIC), 115
neighborhood, 40, 62, 64-66, 73-76
neural network, 94
"noise," 44-45
nonindependence, 67

O
obligor, 16, 24, 101-104, 110, 158, 161-163
Office of Fair Trading (OFT), 174, 176
overcollateralization, 155, 157-158
ownership interest, 156-160

P
pass-through, 78, 140, 154, 156
  senior/subordinated, 149, 173
payment history, 76
predictive model, 65-66
preferred equity, 111, 113
prepayment, 14, 17, 23, 25, 27, 103, 131, 142, 150, 170, 172, 174, 176
principal component, 68-72, 74
private placement, 113

Q
quantitative mapping, 47
quasi-prime, 171-172

R
real estate owned (REO), 162
regression analysis, 69
real estate investment trust (REIT), 154, 159-160
real estate mortgage investment

Index

conduit (REMIC), 138, 156-160
reporting, 17, 22, 85, 100, 110-111, 160
repossession, 11, 18, 110
risk
    future, 15
    grading, 147, 152
    historic, 15
    management, 2, 5, 8, 10, 118, 127, 146, 179
    modeling, 81
    reduction, 10, 12
risk-based
    equity, 128
    pricing, 14-17, 19-21, 23, 25, 27, 145-152
Rule of 78, 104, 172-174, 176

S

scorecard, 9-11, 23, 45-46, 50, 60
scoring, 8, 41-47, 49-51, 53, 55-59, 61-63, 65, 67-69, 71, 73, 75-77, 81, 83, 86, 100, 120, 134, 145-148, 171
seasoning, 20, 23, 72-73, 101, 104, 128, 152, 166
secured credit card, 78-79, 88
securitization, 2, 16, 19, 26, 40, 78, 96, 100, 104, 106-107, 114-116, 119, 127, 130, 138-143, 149, 151-152, 155-159, 161, 163, 166, 173-174
self-certification, 171, 176
senior/subordinated pass-through, 149, 173
service level, 36, 82, 86
severity, 8, 10, 12, 17-18, 20, 22, 26, 100, 103, 132, 135, 148, 178
signal-detection theory, 45

skip tracing, 110
soft-add, 102-103, 110
special-purpose subsidiary (SPS), 158
Standard & Poor's, 127, 144-148

standard variable rate (SVR), 169, 176
static pool analysis, 5, 20, 22-23
surety wrap, 138
surveillance, 17

T

"takedown," 161
target, 6, 15, 88, 139, 178
taxable mortgage pool (TMP), 156-157
teaser, 15, 133
third-party loan, 134

U

up-front fee, 126

V

validity, 41, 43, 76
vendor's single interest (VSI), 102
verification, 102-103, 109, 135, 145

W

warehouse
    lines, 137
    loans, 137
warehousing, 114
weighting, 43, 61, 70, 72
whole-loan mortgage pool, 177
wholesaler, 173

InformationManagementNetwork

Information Management Network Is Committed To Structured Finance!

Over 6000 Professionals Attend Our *Structured Finance Events* Each Year

For Complete Information:
Phone: (212) 768-2800 ext 1 • Fax: (212) 768-2484
Email: mail@imn.org • World Wide Web: www.imn.org